The Papist's Guide to America

by Daniel Schwindt

daniel.schwindt@gmail.com

Contents

Prologue

The Republicans and Democrats are neck-and-neck in their attempts to shower disdain on Pope Francis. Who will come out the victor in this great contest of loathing and condescension?

We could put our money on the Democrats. For example, when the President assembles a pro-choice nun, a gay bishop, and a transvestite to form the Pope's welcoming committee, the message isn't exactly one of hospitality. But what else would we expect from this group, since the whole pro-choice movement, and along with it the politics of subjectivity, is central to their platform?

But the Republicans are no better. Consider "proud Catholic" Congressman Paul Gosar, who loudly boycotted Francis' visit to the United States. Why? Because Francis did not adopt the sanctioned list of Conservative talking points. For example, the Pontiff not only spoke against abortion—but he also expressed concern about the environment. That's how it works in the conservative echo chamber: you take one step off the designated path and you're "one of them"—an alien and an enemy.

Never mind that Francis' two predecessors, Pope Saint John Paul II and Pope Emeritus Benedict XVI, both said the same things about the environment and offered the same warnings. Both of them condemned capitalist market ideology, consumerism, and individualism as values opposed to life. When Francis finally makes the connection between abortion and the "throw-away culture" of capitalism, he is simply reiterating what has already been said. But alas.

If we dare continue through the ranks of the Right, we soon come to the nativist crowd, offended simply at the fact that Francis has the gall to deliver a few speeches during his visit in Spanish. And then of course we can't ignore the standard *Fox News* carnival, exemplified by host Brian Kilmeade (another "proud Catholic"), who said that Francis was "in the wrong country" if he was going to blame money for the problems in the Middle East. America loves capitalism, after all, and according to Kilmeade, Popes are not welcome in the temple of Mammon. We could proceed onward to figures like Rush Limbaugh and his accusations of Marxism, but there is no need.

This sort of bipartisan animosity should give pause to American Catholics, and it has in fact already caused feelings of estrangement.

And so, the purpose of this little book is to act as a guide and a "re-orientation" for the American Catholic, who finds himself increasingly alienated within the American political scene—who watches the building hostility that Pope Francis faces whenever he speaks to Americans about American ways.

Our central thesis is simply this: that this feeling of alienation is not new to American Catholics; that American Catholics have been tolerated in America but never really welcomed; and that the appearance of Pope Francis has only brought certain tensions and animosities to the surface of American political conversation.

Although this seems to bode ill for the American Church, it is actually a gift and an invitation to wake from a century of slumber. We all know that America is dying of spiritual thirst, so to speak, and if the Church carries with it the Living Water, then there is no better time for Catholics to become aware of our situation, and to take action.

What sort of action? Well, it is a second thesis of this book that we not only *can* but in fact *should* look to Pope Francis as our exemplar. It seems to us, in fact, that a very real affection and sense of docility toward the pastoral leadership of our Pope is just the antidote for the ills we have been facing. The reason we say this will be explained in detail below. For now, suffice it to say that Pope Francis has thus far given us nothing but opportunity for inspiration, and he has taught us much about the proper conduct of a Catholic in hostile territory.

Consider his visit to America: By surrounding Francis with sinners, President Obama only managed to make him look more like Jesus Christ, who dined with the sinners, and who loved them. And the Republicans, with all their mocking propaganda, only make themselves look more and more like Pharisees. For the Roman Pontiff, it's clearly a win-win. And all he had to do was show up.

Our purpose here is to call American Catholics to follow his lead: *to show up, and to show up as Catholics without shame or reservation.* Nothing more, nothing less.

As for the structure of the work, we begin with an overview of the American "predicament"—and this is part I. This section gives the reader a concise overview of the history of our present situation. It reads a bit like the biography of an idea—an idea called "Liberalism." The reader already familiar with all aspects of this idea may wish to skip ahead. So be it. Part II lays out the Catholic vision of society, law, and politics. Some of the material here has been reproduced from the author's previous work.[1] Part III acts as a miniature compendium of statements from various popes and provides a "program" of positions on relevant topics. This serves the purpose of a reference for the reader who wishes to follow the lead of the Pontiffs.

---

[1] The sections on Law and the Catholic view of Man have previously appeared in *Catholic Social Teaching: A New Synthesis* by Daniel Schwindt (2015).

I. Predicaments

1. America and the Catholic Church

a. 'Persona non grata'

America is not welcoming to the Catholic. That is to say, the Catholic is *welcome*, but he is not welcome *as a Catholic*. He must check whatever parts of his identity are specifically Catholic at the door if he wishes to thrive. He may "exist," but if he wishes to participate or achieve, he must do so as a spiritual void.

Does this sound like an exaggeration? Let us take a substantial case of Catholic achievement then. A Catholic may even become President, as John F. Kennedy did. But what was the cost? Let's allow him to speak for himself by quoting a speech he presented during his campaign:

> "I am not the Catholic candidate for president. I am the Democratic Party's candidate for president, who happens also to be a Catholic. I do not speak for my church on public matters, and the church does not speak for me...Whatever issue may come before me as president — on birth control, divorce, censorship, gambling or any other subject — I will make my decision...in accordance with what my conscience tells me to be the national interest, and without regard to outside religious pressures or dictates."[2]

The price, for President Kennedy, was nothing less than his Catholic identity. And judging from the fact that many Catholics are proud of these words, or at least see nothing wrong with them, it is clear that we are a nation of Kennedys.

---

[2] *Address to the Greater Houston Ministerial Association* delivered on September 12, 1960 in Houston, TX.

Now compare this to the great Catholic historian, Hilaire Belloc. In 1906 he ran for a seat in the English parliament. His opponent, knowing that Belloc was a devout Catholic and of French blood, made his slogan "Don't vote for a Frenchman and a Catholic." Belloc responded by standing up amidst his Protestant audience and saying:

> "Gentlemen, I am a Catholic. As far as possible, I go to Mass every day. This [taking a rosary out of his pocket] is a rosary. As far as possible, I kneel down and tell these beads every day. If you reject me on account of my religion, I shall thank God that He has spared me the indignity of being your representative."

The audience erupted in applause, and Belloc won the seat. He overwhelmed the prejudices of his audience with his manly authenticity, and the people decided they would rather have a leader in office than a mirror.

Belloc would not compromise his honor to win a vote, and his voters loved him for it. Kennedy, on the other hand, apparently understood that he could not enter an American office at all without first swearing an "oath of inauthenticity," pretending (indeed, we can only hope that he was pretending) to leave his faith on the White House lawn.

First, this should tell us something about our politicians. In the words of C.S. Lewis: "We make men without chests and expect of them virtue and enterprise. We laugh at honour and are shocked to find traitors in our midst. We castrate and bid the geldings be fruitful."

To prefer the mirror is to populate government seats with flatterers and hypocrites, and we end by affirming Nicolas Gomez-Davila, who said: "Democracy is the political regime in which the citizen entrusts the public interests to those men to whom he would never entrust his private interests."[3]

But more than that, this should speak to us about ourselves and to what degree we have been willing to lay aside the Catholic identity in order to bow and scrape before the altars of secularism. We have, in a very real sense, transformed ourselves into a population of unconscious hypocrites.

b. Pope Leo XIII and 'Americanism'

The Church had seen this situation coming and had tried to give warning. On January 22 of 1899, Pope Leo XIII promulgated the Apostolic Letter, *Testem Benevolentiae Nostrae*, subtitled "Concerning new opinions, virtue, nature and grace, with regard to Americanism." It was addressed to Cardinal Gibbons, Archbishop of Baltimore, Baltimore being the premier "see" in the United States. The purpose of the letter was "to call attention to some things to be avoided and corrected,"[4] including but not limited to:

> "the confounding of license with liberty, the passion for discussing and pouring contempt upon any possible subject, the assumed right to hold whatever opinions one pleases upon any subject and to set them forth in print to the world, have so wrapped minds in darkness that there is now a greater need of the Church's teaching office than ever before, lest people become unmindful both of conscience and of duty."[5]

We quote at length this letter because it states plainly the opposition that came into being between the Catholic view and the American one:

[3] Nicolás Gómez Dávila, *Don Colacho's Aphorisms* (Bogotá: Villegas Editores, 2001), p. 153.
[4] *Testem Benevolentiae Nostrae.*
[5] Ibid.

"The underlying principle of these new opinions is that, in order to more easily attract those who differ from her, the Church should shape her teachings more in accord with the spirit of the age and relax some of her ancient severity and make some concessions to new opinions. Many think that these concessions should be made not only in regard to ways of living, but even in regard to doctrines which belong to the deposit of the faith. They contend that it would be opportune, in order to gain those who differ from us, to omit certain points of her teaching which are of lesser importance, and to tone down the meaning which the Church has always attached to them. It does not need many words, beloved son, to prove the falsity of these ideas if the nature and origin of the doctrine which the Church proposes are recalled to mind. The Vatican Council says concerning this point: "For the doctrine of faith which God has revealed has not been proposed, like a philosophical invention to be perfected by human ingenuity, but has been delivered as a divine deposit to the Spouse of Christ to be faithfully kept and infallibly declared. Hence that meaning of the sacred dogmas is perpetually to be retained which our Holy Mother, the Church, has once declared, nor is that meaning ever to be departed from under the pretense or pretext of a deeper comprehension of them." -Constitutio de Fide Catholica, Chapter iv.

"We cannot consider as altogether blameless the silence which purposely leads to the omission or neglect of some of the principles of Christian doctrine, for all the principles come from the same Author and Master, "the Only Begotten Son, Who is in the bosom of the Father."-John i, I8. They are adapted to all times and all nations, as is clearly seen from the words of our Lord to His apostles: "Going, therefore, teach all nations; teaching them to observe all things whatsoever I have commanded you, and behold, I am with you all days, even to the end of the world."-Matt. xxviii, 19. Concerning this point the Vatican Council says: "All those things are to be believed with divine and catholic faith which are contained in the Word of God, written or handed down, and which the Church, either by a solemn judgment or by her ordinary and universal magisterium, proposes for belief as having been divinely revealed."-Const. de fide, Chapter iii.

"Let it be far from anyone's mind to suppress for any reason any doctrine that has been handed down. Such a policy would tend rather to separate Catholics from the Church than to bring in those who differ. There is nothing closer to our heart than to have those who are separated from the fold of Christ return to it, but in no other way than the way pointed out by Christ."

As for the Church's part,

> "she has never neglected to accommodate herself to the character and genius of the nations which she embraces...she has been accustomed to so yield that, the divine principle of morals being kept intact, she has never neglected to accommodate herself to the character and genius of the nations which she embraces.

> "Who can doubt that she will act in this same spirit again if the salvation of souls requires it? In this matter the Church must be the judge, not private men who are often deceived by the appearance of right."

> "...that opinion of the lovers of novelty, according to which they hold such liberty should be allowed in the Church, that her supervision and watchfulness being in some sense lessened, allowance be granted the faithful, each one to

follow out more freely the leading of his own mind and the trend of his own proper activity. They are of the opinion that such liberty has its counterpart in the newly given civil freedom which is now the right and the foundation of almost every secular state."[6]

Clearly this leaves the American Catholic in a difficult position. He is in hostile territory. He is tolerated, but he is not at all comfortable. He may stay so long as he keeps to himself.

Catholics make up 22% of the general population and 30% of Congress, and yet it is abundantly clear that Catholic doctrine has no discernible impact on the government of this nation. This can only mean that the laity in America have agreed to the settlement. They form a giant, but the giant is asleep, neutralized by the secular ideology that encases them. They represent a stockpile of unexploded dynamite at the very base of the idols of Enlightenment, Secularism, and Materialist Humanism. The primary purpose of this book is to initiate a spark. In order to find out how this can be done, let us begin dissecting the American psyche from its formation and up to the present day.

c. American Idiosyncrasies

America is unique in that it illustrates what a society constructed entirely on liberal foundations might actually look like. The same cannot be said of post-Revolutionary France, which had to demolish the *Ancien Regime* before they could implement anything new. Because they could not accomplish this demolition completely, the remains of those pre-existing structures inevitably channeled its development in certain directions. Centralization occurred almost immediately and at an incredibly accelerated rate. The ruins of

---

[6] Ibid.

previous despotism were still accessible, and so the Republican administrators could not help reanimating them:

> "Centralization was raised from its tomb and restored to its place; whence it happened that, all the checks which had formerly served to limit its power being destroyed, and not revived, there sprang out of the bosom of a nation which had just overthrown royalty a power more extensive, more detailed, more absolute than any of our monarchs had ever wielded. The enterprise seemed incredibly bold and unprecedentedly successful, because people only thought of what they saw before them, and forgot the past. The despot fell; but the most substantial portion of his work remained: his administrative system survived his government. And ever since, whenever an attempt has been made to overthrow an absolute government, the head of Liberty has been simply planted on the shoulders of a servile body."[7]

America, on the other hand, did not emanate from the slain corpse of the *Ancien Regime*, but was built almost from the ground up. This is an important distinction because it allows us to understand why the French Republic seemed to plummet directly into unprecedented centralization, while in America, although this same tendency has been present, it has been impeded.

Thus, it has been that the American experiment proceeded along lines of development similar to those of the French Revolution, but more slowly and more observably, which is beneficial for us as sociological researchers. It allows us to dissect this development in all its various aspects.

---

[7] Alexis de Tocqueville, *The Ancien Regime and the Revolution*, 3.8.

11

d. A Fundamental Disharmony

When we peel away the popular names and events of American history—personalities like Washington, Jefferson, and Adams, or symbols like the Statue of Liberty and the Star-Spangled Banner—and reach into the depths of the average man on the street, what do we find there? What are his habits, preconceptions, and prejudices?—his strengths and his limitations?

If one fundamental condition stands out which differentiates us from other societies it is the absence of hierarchical ordering. The principles of the American Revolution, after all, emphasize liberty and equality above all else, and this necessarily kindles a degree of disorder. This is not bad in itself, so long as the element of liberty in society is harmonized with the element of order. When the two elements are properly balanced the society maintains a healthy *stasis* of "ordered liberty." But America, from the beginning, has placed a higher value on freedom than on solidarity, and concerned itself more with ensuring liberties than with erecting cooperative structures to contain it.

This neglect has had consequences. Harmony is the principle of stability. Because we have neglected harmony we tend—both psychologically and socially—to vacillate between extremes. We run to one side and then fall back to the other, never able to find rest. This is because, as the old saying goes, a good thing carried to an extreme—even liberty—becomes its opposite: despotism. And so, as the last two centuries have unfolded we've seen a relentless insistence on liberty with a corresponding centralization of power in the hands of the State. This may seem paradoxical, but it is the fundamental disharmony of those Enlightenment tendencies which so inspired the Founders, who themselves pushed the principle of liberty to its extreme, thereby setting their nation on the path to absolutism as a result.

In America this initial disharmony has given birth to a series of others, which it is the purpose of this chapter to enumerate. They occur in pairs which, although seemingly opposed, are actually complementary, like two sides of a coin or two poles of a loadstone. They are as follows:

- *Individualism and Collectivism*

- *Rationalism and Sentimentalism*

- *Equality and Insecurity*

- *Superiority and Inferiority*

- *Secularism and Civil Religion*

- *Ignorance and Ideology*

e. Individualism and Collectivism

Throughout this section we will refer extensively to the work of Alexis de Tocqueville (1805-1859), for the simple reason that his insights into the American psyche were as unparalleled in his day as they are timely in ours. Even though, it must be admitted, his theological and political opinions were by no means orthodox, this in no way diminishes his value as a descriptive sociologist. He is absolutely indispensable if we wish to understand our intellectual heritage.

With that said, an excellent point of departure for our study might be the following observation on the early development of individualism. According to Tocqueville, the American citizen is usually self-directed and self-reliant—but also self-centered. In his endeavors he "directs all his feelings on to himself alone." Tocqueville explains that although in the past this was called by the name of "egoism" and was considered a vice, it has been transmuted by Americans into a "new idea" called individualism:

> "Individualism is a recently coined expression prompted by a new idea, for our forefathers knew only of egoism.
>
> "Egoism is an ardent and excessive love of oneself which leads man to relate everything back to himself and to prefer himself above everything.
>
> "Individualism is a calm and considered feeling which persuades each citizen to cut himself off from his fellows and to withdraw into the circle of his family and friends in such a way that he thus creates a small group of his own and willingly abandons society at large to its own devices. Egoism springs from a blind instinct; individualism from wrong-headed thinking rather than from depraved feelings. It originates as much from defects of intelligence as from the mistakes of the heart.
>
> "Egoism blights the seeds of every virtue; individualism at first dries up only the source of public virtue. In the longer term it attacks and destroys all the others and will finally merge with egoism."[8]

What Tocqueville observes is that within a context of America, egoism masquerades as a rationally justified philosophy, thereby escaping the negative connotations which were traditionally attached to it. This new form of egoism is then able to become more widespread and accepted, resulting in a reinforced lack of concern for those who are not immediately and unavoidably close to us. This, as we should expect, leads inevitably to social dissolution:

---

[8] *Democracy in America*, 2.2.2.

"Such people owe nothing to anyone and, as it were, expect nothing from anyone. They are used to considering themselves in isolation and quite willingly imagine their destiny as entirely in their own hands. Thus, not only does democracy make men forget their ancestors but also hides their descendants and keeps them apart from their fellows. It constantly brings them back to themselves and threatens in the end to imprison them in the isolation of their own hearts."[9]

Remember that anything carried to the extreme becomes its own opposite. No one can grapple with all of life's questions by himself. He must always look to an external source. This had been the function of the Church and its cumulative Tradition. It was a collective body of wisdom whose purpose was to discern the answers to life's mysteries and then present them to the people in a form they could understand. But under the Liberal regime man is liberated from the Church and left to "judge for himself." He is at first ecstatic and confident, but then he realizes how impossible the task is. Yet *he must* have answers. And so he turns to the only social authority which exists within Liberal democracy: he turns to the general public. He adopts as his own whatever opinion everyone else happens to be holding. As Tocqueville saw:

"Not only is commonly held opinion the only guide to the reason of the individual in democracies but this opinion has, in these nations, an infinitely greater power than in any other. In times of equality, men have no confidence in each other because of their similarities but this very similarity gives them an almost limitless trust in the judgment of the public as a whole. For it appears likely, in their view, that, since they all have similar ideas, truth will reside with the greatest number...

[9] *Ibid.*

"In democratic nations, the general public possesses an unusual power which aristocracies could not imagine. It does not impose its beliefs by persuasion but inserts them in men's souls by the immense pressure of corporate thinking upon the intelligence of each single man.

"In the United States, the majority takes upon itself the task of supplying to the individual a mass of ready-made opinions, thus relieving him of the necessity to take the proper responsibility of arriving at his own."[10]

While such a society is consciously *individualist,* they are unconsciously *collectivist* in their mental processes. And so the first disharmony is established. When a man sets out to judge every matter independently, he simply trades an old authority for a new one—he trades the Church for the masses. In any case, he does not do what he set out to do, which was to judge for himself. All the while he congratulates himself for shrugging off the shackles of old, while at that very moment the crowd begins dictating to him his every notion.

f. Rationalism and Sentimentalism

The second dualism springs from the first: An isolationist attitude implies a strict rationalism:

"I discover that, in the majority of mental processes, each American has but recourse to the individual effort of his own reason. America is thus one of the countries in the world where the precepts of Descartes are least studied and most widely applied. We need not be surprised by that. Americans do not read the works of Descartes because the state of their society diverts them from speculative study and they follow his maxims because it is this very social state

---

[10] Ibid., 2.1.2

which naturally disposes their minds to adopt them. Amid the continuous shifts which prevail in the heart of a democratic society, the bond which unites generations to each other becomes slack or breaks down; each person easily loses the trail of ideas coming from his forbears or hardly bothers himself about them...As for the effect which one man's intelligence can have upon another's, it is of necessity much curtailed in a country where its citizens, having become almost like each other, scrutinize each other carefully and, perceiving in not a single person in their midst any signs of undeniable greatness or superiority, constantly return to their own rationality as to the most obvious and immediate source of truth."[11]

It would be difficult to find a more thoroughgoing rationalism than what Tocqueville has just described. He basically identifies the American philosophic method as unconsciously Cartesian.[12] If man is self-sufficient socially, he must also be self-sufficient in mind. This leads to the identification of the individual reason as an adequate means to discover all truths:

"So, it is not merely trust in any particular individual which is destroyed, but also the predilection to take the word of any man at all. Each man thus retreats into himself from where he claims to judge the world."[13]

If the reason is not able to acquire a certain truth, then the truths are considered unnecessary or else rejected entirely. This has disastrous results when it comes to the teachings of the Church, which are by nature beyond the reach of the individual's unaided rationality:

---

[11] Ibid.
[12] A disciple of Rene Descartes (1596-1650), an Enlightenment philosopher made famous by his contributions to the school of Rationalism. He is most well-known for his motto *"cogito, ergo sum"* ("I think, therefore I am").
[13] Ibid.

"As they realize that, without help, they successfully resolve all the small problems they meet in their practical lives, they easily reach the conclusion that there is an explanation for everything in the world and that nothing is beyond the limits of intelligence. So it is that they willingly deny what they cannot understand; that gives them little faith in the extraordinary and an almost invincible distaste for the supernatural."[14]

Through this insistence that every accepted truth be simple enough for immediate rational comprehension, one might suspect the rule of logic to reign supreme in the New World. Yet it is important to remember that while this attitude is feasible in theory, it has precisely the same results as excessive individualism: the individualist sooner or later, even if unconsciously, begins to rely on others, because the task he set for himself was impossible. He is simply not self-sufficient. It works the same way when he insists on the self-sufficiency of his reason.

Because he simply cannot proceed by logic alone, and at the same time refuses the guidance of traditional sources on the pretext that they are tyrannical and superstitious, he turns to another source, inferior to either reason or superstition, in spite of himself: he turns to emotion. When reason fails—which will be frequent and inevitable—he will be guided by whatever he *feels*. Because he cannot *ascend* into the collective wisdom of the Church, he *descends* into passion and whim. He becomes a *sentimentalist*, which is individualistic rationalism's natural, albeit ironic, point of termination.

---

[14] Ibid.

18

g. *Equality and Insecurity*

Equality is another of the highest values of Liberal philosophy. In fact, if we are to believe Tocqueville, Equality is held to more dearly even than Liberty:

> "I think that democratic communities have a natural taste for freedom: left to themselves, they will seek it, cherish it, and view any privation of it with regret. But for equality, their passion is ardent, insatiable, incessant, invincible: they call for equality in freedom; and if they cannot obtain that, they will call for equality in slavery."[15]

For now, it is not important to judge which of the two values is more important, but simply to acknowledge the esteem for Equality which typically exists in our country. Once that is established, we can proceed to the social consequences this ideal produces once it is actually achieved.

In theory, equality draws men closer together and makes them as brothers politically and, less frequently, economically. But what did Tocqueville observe in practice under the reign of Equality? There are many perspectives he adopted in his vast analysis, but we will look at the most commonplace example, work life. What happens when those people, who must cooperate every day in relationships that are unavoidably hierarchical, attempt to operate on the egalitarian mentality? For example, what happens as the "master" becomes an employer?:

> "His authority over his servants becomes timid and at the same time harsh: he has already ceased to entertain for them the feelings of patronizing kindness which long uncontested power always engenders, and he is surprised that, being changed himself, his servant changes also. He wants his

---

[15] Ibid., 2.2.1.

attendants to form regular and permanent habits, in a condition of domestic service which is only temporary: he requires that they should appear contented with and proud of a servile condition, which they will one day shake off—that they should sacrifice themselves to a man who can neither protect nor ruin them—and in short that they should contract an indissoluble engagement to a being like themselves, and one who will last no longer than they will."[16]

Our concern here is not to argue over whether the master ought to imagine, as he may have done in the past, that his race is superior to that of the servant. Our purpose is rather to stand aloof and discern the outcome of the transition. And that outcome, Tocqueville believed, was a change in the character of the relationship between those who command and those who willingly obey. Obedience, it seemed, changed from an honorable act to a necessary but resented kind of oppression:

"Obedience then loses its moral importance in the eyes of him who obeys; he no longer considers it as a species of divine obligation, and he does not yet view it under its purely human aspect; it has to him no character of sanctity or of justice, and he submits to it as to a degrading but profitable condition... They consent to serve, and they blush to obey; they like the advantages of service, but not the master; or rather, they are not sure that they ought not themselves to be masters, and they are inclined to consider him who orders them as an unjust usurper of their own rights."

Further, because this kind of Equality has been presented to all citizens as a primarily political value, it lends the character of politics to those spheres in which it operates:

---

[16] Ibid., 2.3.5.

"Then it is that the dwelling of every citizen offers a spectacle somewhat analogous to the gloomy aspect of political society. A secret and intestine warfare is going on there between powers, ever rivals and suspicious of one another: the master is ill-natured and weak, the servant ill-natured and intractable; the one constantly attempts to evade by unfair restrictions his obligation to protect and to remunerate—the other his obligation to obey. The reins of domestic government dangle between them, to be snatched at by one or the other. The lines which divide authority from oppression, liberty from license, and right from might, are to their eyes so jumbled together and confused, that no one knows exactly what he is, or what he may be, or what he ought to be."[17]

When all advantages are supposedly leveled and all members of society deemed political equals, the assumption follows that no one owes anyone else anything and any who fell behind did so by their own incompetence. There is no other explanation. This is why our economic mentality holds so tightly to the principle of competition. When all participants in the market are equal, the attitude of "every man for himself" is more difficult to censure because the injustices are veiled. And so this phantom Equality both uplifts the people and, at the same time, dissatisfies and sets each on edge:

"When all the privileges of birth and fortune are abolished, when all professions are accessible to all, and a man's own energies may place him at the top of any one of them, an easy and unbounded career seems open to his ambition, and he will readily persuade himself that he is born to no vulgar destinies. But this is an erroneous notion, which is corrected by daily experience. The same equality which allows every citizen to conceive these lofty hopes, renders all the citizens

---

[17] Ibid.

21

less able to realize them: it circumscribes their powers on every side, whilst it gives freer scope to their desires. Not only are they themselves powerless, but they are met at every step by immense obstacles, which they did not at first perceive. They have swept away the privileges of some of their fellow-creatures which stood in their way, but they have opened the door to universal competition: the barrier has changed its shape rather than its position. When men are nearly alike, and all follow the same track, it is very difficult for any one individual to walk quick and cleave a way through the dense throng which surrounds and presses him. This constant strife between the propensities springing from the equality of conditions and the means it supplies to satisfy them, harasses and wearies the mind."[18]

Tocqueville's observations above are but a picture of what happens when economic relationships come to be viewed as utilitarian contracts between competing political equals. This is not to say that this transformation was not necessary or that it is inferior to what came before. That analysis will come later in this study. At the moment we are only marking the characteristics as they occur. Thus, we need only mark that the normative assumption of Equality is capable of introducing strife and perpetual insecurity into the most mundane of human affairs. In doing so, we mark the third disharmony.

h. Superiority and Inferiority

As we develop this concept of disharmony, which creates in the heart of the American a deep sense of contradiction in his reality, the symptoms become more obvious and acute. Consider our national sense of self-esteem, which is both overconfident and anxious:

---

[18] Ibid., 2.2.8.

"Americans seem irritated by the slightest criticism and appear greedy for praise. The flimsiest compliment pleases them and the most fulsome rarely manages to satisfy them; they plague you constantly to make you praise them and, if you show yourself reluctant, they praise themselves. Doubting their own worth, they could be said to need a constant illustration of it before their eyes. Their vanity is not only greedy, it is also restless and jealous. It grants nothing while making endless demands. It begs one moment and quarrels the next."[19]

We cannot think well of ourselves without reference to someone else. We seem unable to remain confident without an assurance of our dominance in relation to another weaker example:

"If I say to an American that the country he lives in is beautiful, he answers: 'True enough. There is not its like in the world!' I admire the freedom enjoyed by its citizens and he answers: 'Freedom is indeed a priceless gift, but very few nations are worthy of enjoying it.' If I note the moral purity which prevails in the United States, he says: 'I realize that a foreigner, struck by the corruption in all the other nations, will be surprised by this sight.' Finally, I leave him to his self-contemplation; but he comes back at me and refuses to leave me until he has prevailed upon me to repeat what I have just said. A more intrusive and garrulous patriotism would be hard to imagine. It wearies even those who respect it."[20]

To put it in the words of Jacques Maritain, another loving friend of the United States, "the American people are anxious to have their country loved; they need to be loved."[21]

---

[19] Ibid., 2.3.16.
[20] Ibid.
[21] *Reflections on America*, ch. 5.

Tocqueville explained this by saying that Americans have so identified themselves with their nation that in some respects they given themselves up to *de-individuation*, which is a process by which one surrenders his own identity and adopts for himself that of another, usually collective, entity. A commonplace example of this process is when sports fans say "we" when speaking of "their" professional sports team, with which they have no real ties to speak of. This allows for a form of vicarious living through the collective, and it is usually abandoned whenever it stops serving its purpose. For example, when "our" team loses, we switch the pronoun to "they." "They really dropped the ball this weekend," we might say. In this way we quickly dissociate ourselves from the entity for the sake of our self-esteem. But this is not so easily done when it comes to our nation.

We learn that we are Americans from birth; we learn that America is "exceptional" from birth; we learn that we live in the "City on a Hill." We learn to draw self-esteem from this source at every step, as we are reminded that America is "the greatest country on earth." We call this patriotism, but it is more accurately termed nationalism. Patriotism is nationalism veiled with positive rhetoric.

Nationalism is the attitude which Erich Fromm said,

> "is our form of incest, is our idolatry, is our insanity. 'Patriotism' is its cult. It should hardly be necessary to say, that by "patriotism" I mean that attitude which puts the own nation above humanity, above the principles of truth and justice; not the loving interest in one's own nation, which is the concern with the nation's spiritual as much as with its material welfare — never with its power over other nations. Just as love for one individual which excludes the love for others is not love, love for one's country which is not part of one's love for humanity is not love, but idolatrous worship."[22]

24

And what can this be except evidence of a profound insecurity? That is the burden of hubris: it is an impossible weight to carry. If you tell yourself long enough that you are of the "greatest race on earth," then it had better be true, or else your own inner self will deny it. And this is precisely what happens for Americans, and it is why Tocqueville found our patriotism "garrulous" and irritating. He was witnessing a subtle, self-inflicted, nation-wide, inferiority complex.

i. Secularism and Civil Religion

Another problem with living vicariously through another is that the temptation to praise ourselves by praising that "other" is almost irresistible. When we praise ourselves outright, it is usually obvious to all parties involved. But when we praise America or the Denver Broncos, we give the appearance of graciousness; our self-worship is masked, sometimes even from ourselves. In this situation the nation can easily develop into an object of outright devotion.

If that temptation were not enough, there is a further difficulty peculiar to our time. Because we have, intentionally or unintentionally, eradicated the public expression of traditional religions from our society, man's religious propensities are frustrated. He cannot abide by the rule of "private religion" even if he has consented to this arrangement in theory. Yet he has no public idols, icons, or shrines to turn to, for they are forbidden. Images remain, but they are all whitewashed of their sacred character. They are the images of the nation: the Flag, the Statue of Liberty, the various monuments. These are the only idols left, and so he cannot help but redirect his religious impulses onto them. The result is what we call "civil religion," which is what happens when we create a spiritual vacuum in the public sphere.[23] Once secularism is

---

[22] Erich Fromm, *The Sane Society*.
[23] Pope Francis drew together the various elements of this chapter and linked them all to the proliferation of false religions in modern society: "The Catholic

embraced, this process occurs almost by a natural law because religious instinct in man abhors the vacuum.[24]

j. Ignorance and Ideology

Perhaps we could summarize all that has been said above as a comprehensive denial of the nature of the human person with respect to his profound frailty and individual limitations. And nowhere has this denial wrought more havoc than in the realm of knowledge.

When man viewed himself as generally ignorant of most things from the start, which is true of each and every one of us, knowledge was able to maintain a position of authority and to direct the affairs of men. But when Enlightenment rationalism combined with Protestant individualism, ignorance was forgotten. One could not hardly expect the common man to vote, much less interpret ancient scriptures, while also admitting that this same man was almost always incompetent regarding such things. And so, ignorance came to be denied altogether, particularly in regard to our social consciousness of the fact. This caused the power and influence of knowledge evaporate, as evidenced by the treatment of institutions such as the Church, who were the traditional guardians of knowledge (let us not forget that it was the Church who established the universities).

---

faith of many peoples is nowadays being challenged by the proliferation of new religious movements, some of which tend to fundamentalism while others seem to propose a spirituality without God. This is, on the one hand, a human reaction to a materialistic, consumerist and individualistic society, but it is also a means of exploiting the weaknesses of people living in poverty and on the fringes of society, people who make ends meet amid great human suffering and are looking for immediate solutions to their needs. These religious movements, not without a certain shrewdness, come to fill, within a predominantly individualistic culture, a vacuum left by secularist rationalism" (*Evangelii Gaudium*, 63).

[24] Cf. Luke 11:24-26.

At this point I should pause to explain what I mean by the term "ignorance." I do not mean the lack of knowledge plain and simple. That is inevitable, universal, and need not, in itself, do violence to society. On the contrary, if this sort of honest ignorance is acknowledged, it becomes that "Socratic" type of ignorance which is really just the first step on the path toward wisdom. No, what I'm concerned with is an unacknowledged or denied ignorance, the kind which St. Augustine called *opinionativeness* and defined as "imagining oneself to know what one does not know." Thus, when I say that man's ignorance is on the rise, I do not mean that man in general now knows less than he once did. I mean instead that the gap between *what a man knows* and *what he imagines himself to know* is widening.

Remember Tocqueville's observation: "I discover that, in the majority of mental processes, each American has but recourse to the individual effort of his own reason...Each man thus retreats into himself from where he claims to judge the world."[25]

Obviously a man has to entertain an incredible view of his intellectual competence in order to attempt to live this way. In fact, it's impossible—unless you happen to be God:

> "God does not regard the human race collectively. He surveys at one glance and severally all the beings of whom mankind is composed, and he discerns in each man the resemblances which assimilate him to all his fellows, and the differences which distinguish him from them. God, therefore, stands in no need of general ideas; that is to say, he is never sensible of the necessity of collecting a considerable number of analogous objects under the same form for greater convenience in thinking."

---

[25] *Democracy in America,* 2.1.2.

God is enabled to see everything at once and need not formulate "laws" or make use of generalities in order to help him understand the cosmos. Man is not so fortunate:

> "Such is, however, not the case with man. If the human mind were to attempt to examine and pass a judgment on all the individual cases before it, the immensity of detail would soon lead it astray and bewilder its discernment: in this strait, man has recourse to an imperfect but necessary expedient, which at once assists and demonstrates his weakness. Having superficially considered a certain number of objects, and remarked their resemblance, he assigns to them a common name, sets them apart, and proceeds onwards."

In short, man begins to "generalize" about what he sees, in hopes that his generalization will be accurate enough to enable him to comprehend more instances than his limitations will allow. He can formulate laws and make predictions, but they are all loose assumptions, and there will always be exceptions:

> "General ideas are no proof of the strength, but rather of the insufficiency of the human intellect; for there are in nature no beings exactly alike, no things precisely identical, nor any rules indiscriminately and alike applicable to several objects at once. The chief merit of general ideas is, that they enable the human mind to pass a rapid judgment on a great many objects at once; but, on the other hand, the notions they convey are never otherwise than incomplete, and they always cause the mind to lose as much in accuracy as it gains in comprehensiveness."[26]

---

[26] Ibid., 2.1.3.

Democracy, with its emphasis on equality, tends to exacerbate this tendency by the illusion of uniformity it tries to present:

> "The man dwelling in a democracy...is aware of beings about him who are virtually similar; he cannot, therefore, think of any part of the human species without his thought expanding and widening to embrace the whole. Any truth which applies to himself seems to apply equally and similarly to all his fellow citizens and those like him...Thus it is that the need to discover common rules which apply to everything, to include a great number of objects in one category and to explain a collection of facts by one single reason, becomes a burning and often blinding passion of the human mind."[27]

Led by this "blinding passion," men engage in an anxious "search for general ideas with whose help they congratulate themselves on being able to depict huge objects at little expense."[28]

In this way man attempts to make straight all the crooked paths. But there is an aphorism that says: "every straight line leads right to a hell."[29] You cannot press reality, with all of its mystery and contradiction, into a comfortably comprehensible set of generalities to be understood and applied with ease. You can try, and you may even succeed in approximating truth with some regularity—but pushed too far this insistence on simplification can only mutilate the truth by forcing it through a net of generalities.

We can now speak properly of the problem of ideology in America. Ideology is just another word for what we've been speaking of: "nets of generalities through which reality is forced for the sake of simplification and at the sacrifice of truth." Ideologies give the

---

[27] Ibid.
[28] Ibid.
[29] Nicolas Gomez-Davila, *Scholia to an Implicit Text*, II.

"believer" a set of explanations which, under the guise of "common sense," pretend to explain every question that comes to him, down to the most complex phenomena. That is why they are so incredibly popular in ages where men who do not know are told they must behave as if they did.

In our day, the ideology market is plentiful: Capitalism is an ideology. Socialism is an ideology. Some have even called our period "The Age of Ideology," and rare is the man who does not use its sieve to mutilate his reality.

To immunize ourselves, we ought to repeat always the advice of H.L. Mencken: "For every subtle and complicated question, there is a perfectly simple and straightforward answer, which is wrong."

k. "Common Sense" and Anti-Intellectualism

Not every man is a philosopher, to be sure, but every man is the student of a philosopher. This holds true whether he knows it or not, and whether he likes it or not. It simply cannot be helped. And so those modern men who claim simplicity are usually claiming their unconscious allegiance to some philosopher they've never heard of and whose influence is all the more powerful for the fact of its being denied. Every day I encounter apostles of Nietzsche, and some specialize further and follow instead Ayn Rand. And virtually all of these follow John Locke, even though few even know his name. And so it is that what passes for common sense, we would be surprised to discover, is not common sense to most people outside our geographical vicinity, and not common sense to anyone outside of our historical vicinity. Our common sense turns out not to be common at all, and far from being the result of some universal human intuition, is the result of some philosopher's novel speculations, put forth, slowly taking root, and spreading on to the "third and fourth generations," which is approximately the length of time it takes for philosophical notions to become the unconscious premises of the man on the street.

The only thing that can save this world from insanity is a harmonious vision capable of lending structure and stability to civilization. So long as we believe that every proposition should be "self-evident," should be "intuitive," should fit neatly into our preconceptions and so feel like "common sense," we will be invincibly ignorant of higher truths. Among these are the truths of the Church in particular, because they cannot be forced into the individualistic, rationalistic mold. Her truths are ordered not to the mind of man, but to eternity—and eternity is not a common sense proposition.

2. The Rise and Fall of Liberalism

a. The Liberal Consensus

Having traced—very roughly—the development of the American mind according to Alexis de Tocqueville, we should now state clearly that we have not been outlining some unique and idiosyncratic social phenomenon. Rather, we have been tracing the American manifestation of the ideology of Liberalism.

Loud and clear we proclaim it: Liberalism, as we have described it in the foregoing pages, neatly summarizes the philosophical consensus of the modern United States. Its premises and values go to form the context in which we all live and work, as well as the pseudo-religious creed under which we worship. It forms our institutions and dictates the unconscious principles from which we reason; and this is true whether or not we acknowledge our allegiance to its precepts. Our consent was implicit simply by our birth in this historical period and in this hemisphere.

This reality—*our reality*—becomes all the more important if we allow ourselves to admit that Liberalism is also the most significant and far-reaching heresy in the history of Christianity, if we may make such a judgment based on the amount of energy and ink the Church has spent waging war against it. Add to that the magnitude of the damages and divisions left in the aftermath, and the judgment becomes undeniable. Thus, any discussion of the Catholic Church's relationship to the modern world must begin and end with the ideology of Liberalism.

Yet this presents an immediate difficulty because the philosophy of Liberalism, as it was originally developed during the Enlightenment period, and as it was immediately rejected by the Church, means something quite different than it is taken to mean in contemporary American speech. Here and now, the word has come to refer more or less to the political platform espoused by the Democratic Party. While this is true in part, because many of the policies of the "Left" are indeed products of Liberalism, it is also misleading, because in some ways its policies are not "liberal" at all. The issue becomes even more confused by the fact that, in opposition to the platform of the Left, we are offered an opposing platform labelled "conservative" and proffered by those calling themselves Republicans. Yet, truth be told, many of the ideas contained in this second set are just as much in the spirit of Liberalism as those of the first.

Obviously, if what has been said above is true, then both of these parties contradict themselves. And this is why it is so essential to restore to the term Liberalism its proper meaning before we go any further. If we can achieve this task, the reader will be enabled, from the start, to overcome two great obstacles which stand in the way of his study of the Catholic's relationship with America:

First, he will discover that the two parties listed on his ballot sheet every four years are, from a philosophical standpoint, blatantly incoherent in their policies and propositions. Second, he will see that, rather than being diametrically opposed, they are in fact two "sects" within the creed of Liberalism.

b. *The Meaning of Liberalism*

Let us begin with the term itself. The word *liberal* is merely a derivation from the Latin *liber*, meaning "free." In this respect it is a fairly innocuous thing. However, since the eighteenth century "the word has been applied more and more to certain tendencies in the intellectual, religious, political, and economical life, which implied partial or total emancipation of man from the supernatural, moral, and Divine order."[30]

This "new form of Liberalism" received its most significant development through the Enlightenment, but to focus on this movement alone would be a mistake of oversimplification: it had its parallels in the religious and economic fields as well (represented by the Reformation and Capitalism, respectively).

The proponents of the new Liberalism argued for a very specific set of principles which, although radical at the time, are now universally recognizable: "unrestrained freedom of thought, religion, conscience, creed, speech, press, and politics."[31] The consequences which naturally follow from these are:

> "on the one hand, the abolition of the Divine right and of every kind of authority derived from God; the relegation of religion from the public life into the private domain of one's individual conscience; the absolute ignoring of Christianity and the Church as a public, legal, and social institution; on the other hand, the putting into practice of the absolute

---

[30] Gruber, H. (1910). "Liberalism," *The Catholic Encyclopedia*. New York: Robert Appleton Company. Retrieved October 15, 2014 from New Advent: http://www.newadvent.org/cathen/09212a.htm

[31] Ibid.

autonomy of every man and citizen, along all lines of human activity, and the concentration of all public authority in one 'sovereignty of the people.' "[32]

Through this development, the term *liberal* transformed from an innocuous adjective and became a fully-fledged "-*ism*," which would in turn become the defining heresy of the modern period. It was against this profound shift that the Church was destined to expend vast energies doing battle. In fact, from the mid-19th century onward there have been so many warnings, refutations, and condemnations of these principles that to list them all would be unfeasible. Limiting ourselves to only the most significant documents in this vein, we are still left with a considerable corpus: *Mirare Vos* (Gregory XVI, 1832), *Quanta cura* (Pius IX, 1864), *Immortale Dei* (Leo XIII, 1885), *Libertas Praestantissimum* (Leo XIII, 1888), *Lamentabili Sane* (St. Pius X, 1907), *Quas Primas* (Pius XI, 1925), *Humani Generis* (Pius XII, 1950).

c. Too Close for Comfort

Because Liberalism is the context into which most of us were born, we might at first be taken aback by the suggestion that these precepts which we now treasure have been tirelessly condemned by one pope after another. We might struggle to understand why Liberalism is an evil at all. Its teachings are indeed so familiar to us that not only can we not imagine why they might be harmful, but we cannot even conceive of any alternative arrangement.

Were we not imbibed with such tenets as "free speech" and "freedom of the press" with our mothers' milk? And yet, in the course of our study, we will encounter statements such as the following from Pope Leo XIII:

---

[32] Ibid.

"We must now consider briefly liberty of speech, and liberty of the press. It is hardly necessary to say that there can be no such right as this, if it be not used in moderation, and if it pass beyond the bounds and end of all true liberty. For right is a moral power which - as We have before said and must again and again repeat - it is absurd to suppose that nature has accorded indifferently to truth and falsehood, to justice and injustice. Men have a right freely and prudently to propagate throughout the State what things soever are true and honorable, so that as many as possible may possess them; but lying opinions, than which no mental plague is greater, and vices which corrupt the heart and moral life should be diligently repressed by public authority, lest they insidiously work the ruin of the State...If unbridled license of speech and of writing be granted to all, nothing will remain sacred and inviolate; even the highest and truest mandates of natures, justly held to be the common and noblest heritage of the human race, will not be spared. Thus, truth being gradually obscured by darkness, pernicious and manifold error, as too often happens, will easily prevail. Thus, too, license will gain what liberty loses; for liberty will ever be more free and secure in proportion as license is kept in fuller restraint."[33]

And what of the "separation of church and state," which is a practical reality, if not the acknowledged consensus, of both parties in America? To this we may return again to Leo:

"[C]ivil society must acknowledge God as its Founder and Parent, and must obey and reverence His power and authority. Justice therefore forbids, and reason itself forbids, the State to be godless; or to adopt a line of action which would end in godlessness-namely, to treat the various

---

[33] *Libertas*, 23.

religions (as they call them) alike, and to bestow upon them promiscuously equal rights and privileges."[34]

Even popular sovereignty seems unable to pass the muster of the pontiff:

> "Amongst these principles the main one lays down that as all men are alike by race and nature, so in like manner all are equal in the control of their life…In a society grounded upon such maxims all government is nothing more nor less than the will of the people, and the people, being under the power of itself alone, is alone its own ruler…The sovereignty of the people…is held to reside in the multitude; which is doubtless a doctrine exceedingly well calculated to flatter and to inflame many passions, but which lacks all reasonable proof…whence it necessarily follows that all things are as changeable as the will of the people, so that risk of public disturbance is ever hanging over our heads."[35]

These sentiments are understandably difficult to swallow. But if we take a moment and open ourselves to the reasoning of the Magisterium, granting her the benefit of the doubt that she rightly deserves as *Mater et Magistra*,[36] at the same time adopting the spirit of *docility*[37] to which we are called, we might find that we are offered a collection of truths which we never thought we needed.

d. The Nature of the Heresy

To understand the problem of Liberalism we need to identify the evil inherent in every heresy.

---

[34] Ibid., 21.
[35] *Immortale Dei*, 26, 31.
[36] Literally, "Mother and Teacher."
[37]*Catechism of the Catholic Church*, 87: "Mindful of Christ's words to his apostles: 'He who hears you, hears me', the faithful receive with docility the teachings and directives that their pastors give them in different forms."

In *Faust*, Goethe has the devil say: "I am a part of the part, that once was a whole."[38] A better definition of heresy could not be found, for each one is not a lie, but is rather a partial truth wrenched away from the whole and then carried off into isolation where it is made into a little god. This is why Belloc said that "heresies survive by the truths they retain." It follows naturally then that if the "truth retained" is of the highest sort, all the more difficult will it be to differentiate it from the original. For although a spark is merely a fragment of the fire, if it is bright enough it may hypnotize the eye long enough to draw it away from the source, even though it presents an inferior glow.

And the partial truth retained in Liberalism?—It was the simple acknowledgement that man is created to be *free*. This in itself is nothing alien to the Church. In fact, it is the oldest and most treasured doctrine of the faith. But through liberalism it was torn from the overarching context of the Church. "Liberty" was then exalted to the status of an end in itself—not just *one truth among* many about man, but *the* truth. Not just one value in a hierarchy of values, but the supreme value, absolute and overshadowing all others. This was a separation of "the part from the whole," and the truth cannot survive the procedure. The life-giving arms of the Church provide a larger context which not only gives direction to man's freedom, but harmonizes it with the supreme truth that is God. Without this, freedom is destined to become a perversion. This is why the Gospels say that *only through the truth shall we be set free*.[39] We are given no reason to believe that liberty can be had otherwise.

And so, as Paul VI recalled in his 1971 Apostolic Exhortation, *Octogesima Adveniens*, "at the very root of philosophical liberalism

---

[38] *Faust*, part I-iii, 1349.
[39] *John* 8:32.

37

is an erroneous affirmation of the autonomy of the individual in his activity, his motivation and the exercise of his liberty."[40]

It was not in holding high man's capacity for liberty that men went wrong, but in carrying this single fragment into isolation and attempting to discard any overarching principle beside it. The Church, seeing this, chose precisely the same imagery as Goethe to identify the unfortunate path that men were taking:

> "[M]any there are who follow in the footsteps of Lucifer, and adopt as their own his rebellious cry, 'I will not serve'; and consequently substitute for true liberty what is sheer and most foolish license. Such, for instance, are the men belonging to that widely spread and powerful organization, who, usurping the name of liberty, style themselves liberals."[41]

e. Three Heads of the Hydra

As suggested above, it is dangerously naïve to entertain a view of Liberalism that recognizes only its political expression. The movement invaded political philosophy, to be sure, but at the same time it reached both above and below that level, disturbing not only the mind of man, but also his body and soul. With its withering touch it dictated anew, not only how he would earn his daily bread, but even how he would relate to the sacred.

Consider for a moment that the heart of Liberalism is an exaggerated notion of human autonomy, which always carries with it, sometimes unconsciously, an unprecedented optimism about the mental aptitudes of the individual. If we survey the last several centuries, do we find corresponding movements within the religious, economic, and political spheres which all manifest this mentality?

---

[40] *Octogesima Adveniens*, 35.
[41] *Libertas*, 14.

Indeed, the task is too easy: The Reformation was nothing more than individualism of religion, transferring to the judgment the individual the weightiest of all tasks—the interpretation of both Scripture and Tradition. In the economic sphere, it is obviously Capitalism that represents an unrestrained embrace of individualism and liberty through the doctrines of sanctioned self-interest and "free markets." And we have just finished describing precepts which, through the Enlightenment, expressed the same symptoms in the political realm: free speech, absolute rights, and secularism.

To confirm the links between these three, we will pause briefly to comment on each.

f. The Reformation

If we understand Liberalism to be an error of reduction, severing branch from vine,[42] then it does not take an extensive argument to show that Luther's three *solas* unquestionably fit the bill. How else can we interpret *sola fide* ("faith alone"), *sola scriptura* ("scripture alone"), and *sola gratia* ("grace alone") than as partial selections of a pre-existent whole? The atomized nature of these doctrines is itself implicit in the term, *sola*. They are the tenets of *nothing-but-ness*. Add to this doctrinal oversimplification the principle of private interpretation, and the concept of authority evaporates taking all hopes of traditional unity along with it.

Here we may draw benefit from a small work by Fr. Felix Sarda y Salvany, published in 1886 under the title *El Liberalismo es Pecado*, or "Liberalism is a Sin." This thin volume meticulously and passionately refutes the errors associated with religious Liberalism.

But first, in case the bluntness of its title and the relative obscurity of its author give pause to the cautious reader, we should mention that it was initially intercepted by a Bishop of liberal opinions, who

---

[42] *John* 15:5.

then submitted it to the Sacred Congregation of the Index, in hopes that the work would be put under ban. The Sacred Congregation reviewed the submission and responded on January 10, 1887 as follows: "not only is nothing found contrary to sound doctrine, but its author, D. Felix Sarda, merits great praise for his exposition and defense of the sound doctrine therein set forth with solidity, order and lucidity, and without personal offense to anyone."

Thus reassured of its orthodoxy, we may comfortably cite from its pages and hear what case it brings against Luther's movement:

> "Rejecting the principle of authority in religion, [Protestantism] has neither criterion nor definition of faith. On the principle that every individual or sect may interpret the deposit of Revelation according to the dictates of private judgment, it gives birth to endless differences and contradictions. Impelled by the law of its own impotence, through lack of any decisive voice of authority in matters of faith, it is forced to recognize as valid and orthodox any belief that springs from the exercise of private judgment. Therefore does it finally arrive, by force of its own premises, at the conclusion that one creed is as good as another; it then seeks to shelter its inconsistency under the false plea of liberty of conscience. Belief is not imposed by a legitimately and divinely constituted authority, but springs directly and freely from the unrestricted exercise of the individual's reason or caprice upon the subject matter of Revelation. The individual or sect interprets as it pleases—rejecting or accepting what it chooses. This is popularly called liberty of conscience. Accepting this principle, Infidelity, on the same plea, rejects all Revelation, and Protestantism, which handed over the premise, is powerless to protest against the conclusion; for it is clear that one who, under the plea of rational liberty, has the right to repudiate any part of

Revelation that may displease him, cannot logically quarrel with one who, on the same ground, repudiates the whole. If one creed is as good as another, on the plea of rational liberty, on the same plea, no creed is as good as any. Taking the field with this fatal weapon of Rationalism, Infidelity has stormed and taken the very citadel of Protestantism, helpless against the foe of its own making."[43]

If we were to characterize the gist of this reasoning, it is that a process which begins in disintegration must proceed toward disorder and terminate in death. Neither can this argument be called a "slippery slope," for he was not conjecturing wildly about what *might happen*, but was observing what *already had*. He was merely connecting dots.

"Such is the mainspring of the heresy constantly dinned into our ears, flooding our current literature and our press. It is against this that we have to be perpetually vigilant, the more so because it insidiously attacks us on the grounds of *a false charity and in the name of a false liberty…*

"The principle ramifies in many directions, striking root into our domestic, civil, and political life, whose vigor and health depend upon the nourishing and sustaining power of religion. For religion is the bond which unites us to God, the Source and End of all good; and Infidelity, whether virtual, as in Protestantism, or explicit, as in Agnosticism, severs the bond which binds men to God and *seeks to build human society on the foundations of man's absolute independence.*"[44]

---

[43] *Liberalismo es Pecado*, ch. 2.
[44] Ibid., emphasis mine.

41

g. The Enlightenment

In much the same way that Luther could be considered the father of the Reformation, John Locke (1632-1704) has been considered the father of political Liberalism. He was the most influential thinker to come from the Enlightenment, and was the philosopher of choice for revolutionaries such as the American Founders.

And what were the "foundations" which Locke laid? For our purposes here we will adopt Christopher Ferrara's summary:[45]

- A hypothetical "social compact" or contract as the foundation of the State.

- The origin of political sovereignty in the "consent" of the governed (invariably presumed to have been given by those who happen to be wielding power).

- "Government by the people" according to the "sovereignty of the people," meaning strict majority rule on all questions, including the most profound moral ones.

- Church-State separation and the non-"interference" of religion in politics.

- The confinement of religion, above all the revealed truths of Christianity, to the realm of "private" opinions and practices one is free to adopt (or to denounce) if it pleases him, but which are to have no controlling effect on law or public policy.

- The unlimited pursuit of gain, including the freedom to buy, sell and advertise anything whatsoever the majority deems permissible by law.

---

[45] Christopher A. Ferrara, *Liberty, the god that failed: policing the sacred and constructing the myths of the secular state from Locke to Obama.* Angelico Press (Tacoma, 2012). p. 15.

- Total liberty of thought and action, both private and public, within the limits of a merely external "public peace" essentially reduced to the protection of persons and property from invasion by others—in sum, a "free-market society."

- The dissolubility of marriage, and thus the family, as a mere civil contract founded on a revocable consent.

These principles found their most absolute expression in the French Revolution. The American Revolution, however, suffices as another clear example, and the Declaration of Independence acts as a neat summary of Locke's ideas. This should come as no surprise, since the Declaration was penned by Jefferson who was so enamored with Locke that he added his bust to a special canvas alongside Francis Bacon and Isaac Newton. These, he wrote, were "the three greatest men that have ever lived, without any exception...having laid the foundation of those superstructures which have been raised."[46]

h. Capitalism

That Capitalism is an expression of Liberalism should be painfully obvious by now. To illustrate the point further, however, we might take Milton Friedman, economic advisor to Ronald Reagan and internationally known proponent of laissez-fair economic policy. In his 1962 book titled *Capitalism and Freedom*, he wrote that "the intellectual movement that went under the name of liberalism emphasized freedom as the ultimate goal and the individual as the ultimate entity in the society."[47] This movement "supported laissez-faire at home as a means of reducing the role of the state in economic affairs and thereby enlarging the role of the individual."[48] Friedman thus considered himself a thoroughgoing Liberal, as much as this might dismay his contemporary disciples. But the only reason

---

[46] *Letter to John Trumbull*, Thomas Jefferson: Writings, 939.
[47] Milton Friedman, *Capitalism and Freedom*.
[48] Ibid.

for this dismay is that Friedman was consistent; our contemporaries are not.

At this point we do not intend to examine the policies or problems associated with Capitalism. We will spend a great deal of time on this subject as we progress further into our study. Here it will suffice to show what philosophical wellspring fed Capitalism in its beginnings, because that source has since been veiled by our confused terminology. If we had not taken care to clear this up, the phrasing used in many encyclicals and documents would have been impossible for us to properly grasp. For example, when Pope Pius XI applauds "boldly breaking through the confines imposed by liberalism,"[49] and John XXIII condemns "unrestricted competition in the liberal sense,"[50] they are speaking with a unified voice of Capitalism.[51]

i. The Dust Settles

By the time this threefold deluge had run its course over the surface of the West, nothing recognizable remained of the old structures. As the waters fell, the Church settled down, like Noah's ark, on a mountain top, left alive but dry-docked, able to survey the damage but powerless to speak or act any longer against it. How different this was from the situation of Pope Gelasius who in 494 had been able to write to the emperor himself:

> "There are two powers, august Emperor, by which this world is chiefly ruled, namely, the sacred authority of the priests and the royal power. Of these that of the priests is the more weighty, since they have to render an account for even the kings of men in the divine judgment. You are also aware, dear son, that while you are permitted honorably to rule

---

[49] *Quadragesimo Anno*, 25.
[50] *Mater et Magistra*, 23.
[51] See also: *Sollicitudo rei Socialis*, 20, 21, and 41.

over human kind, yet in things divine you bow your head humbly before the leaders of the clergy."[52]

But now all future princes were to be caste in the mold of Henry VIII—answerable to no one but themselves and ready to form their own doctrines according to convenience and fancy, an act which Luther's example had justified in advance. Scripture itself, that great treasure assembled and safeguarded by the Church through the centuries, had been wrenched from her grip and distributed *en masse* to be subjected to every interpretive novelty.

It has been frequently suggested that the Church should have embraced this new position outside of all temporal powers, and that She should not *need* involvement with worldly powers in order to reach the lives of men. But this is all to miss the point: no one has ever said that the Church *required* an acknowledged position of social authority in order to survive. It is clear that She has survived and will continue to survive without it. The question is not whether She "needs the help" of the temporal powers in order to thrive, but whether or not the temporal powers need Her. The cries and condemnations of the Church were not those of jealousy but of concern, warnings of the wolves closing in.

j. Orthodoxy and Heresy Rendered Incomprehensible

To say that this revolution changed man to his core—that it modified the way he sees Truth itself—sounds a bit drastic. Yet consider the way in which we imagine, or, more accurately, are no longer capable of imagining, traditional concepts such as *heresy*.

Heresy, from an etymological standpoint, means nothing more than "to choose for oneself." Obviously, then, the word is entirely appropriate for one who departs from orthodoxy to blaze his own trail. Heresy, then, implies the existence of orthodoxy, which is its

---

[52] Pope Gelasius I to Emperor Anastasius in 494.

counterpart. In the past, every heretic believed himself to be orthodox. The two terms are related to one another, in the same way that "to be inside" of something implies the existence of an "outside." But with Liberalism something altogether new was introduced to man. It was a heresy, to be sure, but for the first time it was a heresy that made no pretenses at orthodoxy. It was, in fact, the first heresy to more or less explicitly reject orthodoxy *as a valid conception*. And because orthodoxy signifies *those beliefs which are true*, to render it invalid is to render incomprehensible the traditional notions about truth and error.

To quote again from Fr. Sarda:

> "Liberalism...transgresses all commandments. To be more precise: in the doctrinal order, Liberalism strikes at the very foundations of faith; it is heresy radical and universal, because *within it are comprehended all heresies...*"[53]

> "It repudiates dogma altogether and substitutes opinion, whether that opinion be doctrinal or the negation of doctrine. Consequently, it denies every doctrine in particular. If we were to examine in detail all the doctrines or dogmas which, within the range of Liberalism, have been denied, we would find every Christian dogma in one way or another rejected—from the dogma of the Incarnation to that of Infallibility."[54]

But Fr. Sarda will not leave his analysis incomplete. The explicit denial of the legitimacy of dogma carries with it an implicit affirmation of a "new dogma" which is both universal and negative in its character:

---

[53] *Liberalismo es Pecado*, Fr. Felix Sarda y Salvany, ch. 3.
[54] *Liberalismo es Pecado*, Fr. Felix Sarda y Salvany, ch. 3.

"Nonetheless Liberalism is in itself dogmatic; and it is in the declaration of its own fundamental dogma, the absolute independence of the individual and the social reason, that it denies all Christian dogmas in general. Catholic dogma is the authoritative declaration of revealed truth—or a truth consequent upon Revelation—by its infallibly constituted exponent. This logically implies the obedient acceptance of the dogma on the part of the individual and of society. Liberalism refuses to acknowledge this rational obedience and denies the authority. It asserts the sovereignty of the individual and social reason and enthrones Rationalism in the seat of authority. It knows no dogma except the dogma of self-assertion. Hence it is heresy, fundamental and radical, the rebellion of the human intellect against God."[55]

The victory of liberalism meant the extinction of the concepts of both heresy *and* orthodoxy, which really represented nothing more than the primordial duality of *truth* and *falsity*. The old positive-negative pair was then replaced with a single, universal negative which rendered the previous paradigm illegitimate and, further, assured that anyone indoctrinated into the negative dogma of liberalism would be completely unable to understand the old terms. Man was left to sit alone in the privacy of his home, asking with Pilate "What is truth?"[56]

k. Vatican II and the New Era

The Gates of Hell will not prevail against the Church, but we're given no guarantee that the Church will prevail in every single battle. In the words of J.R.R. Tolkien, we are engaged in "the long defeat." This puts the Church in an interesting position. The Apostles were instructed that, if rejected, they should shake the dust

---

[55] Ibid.
[56] John 18:38.

from their feet and move to the next city; but the Church may never do this. Her assigned city is the world. She is with man until the end, for that is her entire purpose. So what is the proper course?

The Church is an *expert in humanity*.[57] She is its physician, and a responsible physician, if he senses the danger of disease or infection, does everything he can to warn his patient of the threat. Ideally speaking, his advice will be heeded (he is the expert, after all) and the patient's health will be maintained. But sometimes, as we all know from our own experiences, the patient disregards his doctor's advice and contracts the disease in spite of the efforts of his advisor. In this case and at this point, his doctor will accept this change in conditions and readjust his treatment. We would call him obstinate, ineffective, and even unwise if he did not make this change, for the disease has now set in and this requires *advice of a different kind*. The patient is diseased. The physician must treat him accordingly, and no amount of lecture about what he could have done to prevent the infection will be of any use to anyone: that course is not currently open to either party.

To put it another way, the Good Shepherd does everything he possibly can to keep his flock together. However, should the wolves scatter the sheep, he will, if he is indeed the Good Shepherd, travel far and wide to recover those who have wandered away. If they have wandered into the desert, the bog, or the forest, he goes there, and he goes not because he wishes it or because he enjoys the bog, but because that is where the sheep have gone.

We must keep this in mind as we approach the most significant Magisterial result of the Liberal revolution: The Second Vatican Council. Also called Vatican II, this event was nothing more or less than the decision of the Church to enter the bog of modernism, so to

---

[57] *CSDC*, 61.

speak. Like the Good Shepherd and the Good Doctor, she chose this path not because it was good, but because Her vocation required it.

Formally opened by Pope John XXIII on October 11, 1962 and closed under Pope Paul VI in 1965, this twenty-first ecumenical council of the Church was precisely the sort of action described above. The Church had made every effort to administer preventative treatment and curb the infection at its source. It had made war on man's behalf for over 100 years on the Liberal contagion, but to no avail. Western Civilization was now diseased, and so a new form of counsel was necessary.

It is important to remember what was said earlier regarding concepts like "orthodoxy" and "heresy," that they had been rendered incomprehensible to the modern man. A person born and raised in the Liberal context cannot understand why he must believe something any more than why he must not. Everything must pass through the lens of "freedom" which is the only discerning lens his cultural training provided him with. This ensures that those old notions do not compute.

Sensing this, the Church called together its best physicians from around the world in order to discern the idiosyncrasies of man's new condition—in body, mind and soul. How has he faired throughout the revolution? In what ways has he been affected? What are his symptoms? And what sort of treatment can best bring him back to health?

1. Continuity and Renewal

Before we discuss the actual outcome of the Council and the responses it provoked, something must be said for the nature of the Church's mission.

The Church is tasked with protecting the eternal and unchanging teachings of the Church, but at the same time she must provide appropriate adaptations, and, when necessary, *re-adaptations*, for each society and historical period. The Church must "become all things to all people," and this means that when a new epoch presents itself, altering custom, language, and thought, it is up to the Church to make sure that the presentation and application are still true to the Tradition. This necessitates that the Church adopt a twofold method in regard to its message:

On the one hand it is constant, for it remains identical in its fundamental inspiration, in its "principles of reflection," in its "criteria of judgment," in its basic "directives for action," and above all in its vital link with the Gospel of the Lord. On the other hand, it is ever new, because it is subject to the necessary and opportune adaptations suggested by the changes in historical conditions and by the unceasing flow of the events which are the setting of the life of people and society.[58]

The Church speaks with a voice that is "consistent and at the same time ever new."[59] This is absolutely not a question of *relevance*. Relevance comes down to a matter of whim and attempts to achieve it often amount to self-compromise and an appeal to changing whims. The Church does not sacrifice at that altar.

It is a question of distinguishing *principles* from their concrete *application*: Principles are unchanging and eternal, but a particular application of a principle may not be appropriate for each and every historical circumstance. The Sun casts light on a different portion of the earth's surface every hour; but does this mean that the Sun is on the move? On the contrary, it is we who are constantly in flux, and if the Light of the Church appears to alter itself, it is only in accordance with the inconstancies of the world. Loud and clear it must be proclaimed: when the Church demands something which

---

[58] *SRS*, 3.
[59] CiV, 12.

appears different today than what it asked yesterday, this should not be taken as contradiction—much less should it be assumed that the Church is "admitting error" and "correcting its mistakes." It is simply evidence for us of a changing world. More importantly, it is proof of a Living, Teaching Church.

m. Outcomes of the Council

By the time the doors closed on Vatican II, the members had produced four *constitutions*, three *declarations*, and nine *decrees*. Each of these has its purpose, although opinions seem to vary as to the exact significance of each. What is generally acknowledged, however, is that their doctrinal significance is hierarchical, with the constitutions acting as the most binding of the three, while the remaining two categories are of less gravity, aimed at addressing certain specific concerns or acting as appendices to a constitution.

We cannot go into depth here on each document that was produced, so instead we will mention only the declaration *Dignitatis Humanae*, which turned out to be one of the most divisive of the collection. It therefore serves as an appropriate illustration for us, because the arguments presented for or against it tend to be representative of the entire debate regarding the Council.

Dignitatis Humanae has generated a great deal of argument and debate for such a concise document. It is only a few pages long, so the reader cannot be excused from obtaining a copy for examination. This document, called the "Declaration on Religious Freedom," addresses the relationship between the Church and modern states, as well as between modern states and the individual.

In brief, the document states that "all men are to be immune from coercion on the part of individuals or of social groups and of any human power, in such wise that no one is to be forced to act in a manner contrary to his own beliefs, whether privately or publicly, whether alone or in association with others, within due limits."[60] But its authors take care from the first paragraph to say that this document "leaves untouched traditional Catholic doctrine on the moral duty of men and societies toward the true religion and toward the one Church of Christ."[61]

Now it is understandable that those who have read and treasured the encyclicals of Leo XIII and predecessors would be at first confused at these two statements placed right next two each other. After all, we find there that "the State, constituted as it is, is clearly bound to act up to the manifold and weighty duties linking it to God, by the public profession of religion…it is a public crime to act as though there were no God. So, too, is it a sin for the State not to have care for religion as something beyond its scope, or as of no practical benefit."[62] Does the declaration of Vatican II contradict this saying?—and, if so, which is the faithful Catholic to accept?

But at this point we must marshal before us what was said above: that the whole purpose of Vatican II, and any other council for that matter, was to provide at the same time *continuity and renewal* of the unchanging truths of the Christian Tradition. It is entirely superficial to read the anti-Liberal documents of the warrior popes such as Leo XIII and the three Piuses in precisely the same fashion and from the same point of view as the documents of Vatican II. Remember the role of the physician before and after the disease has set in: Leo XIII was trying, until the very last moment, to prevent the spread of the infection. He was trying to save the progression of the illness from entering a new stage. He and his predecessors did not succeed. So be it. The illness spread through the world and changed its character entirely. The *good physician*, tender and

---

[60] *Dignitatis Humanae*, 2.
[61] Ibid., 1.
[62] *Immortale Dei*, 6.

faithful, convened the Council in order to reassess and formulate the new treatment.

In its assessment, the Council found that it now existed on the outskirts of secular societies, individualistic in mentality, obsessed with rights, and largely unable to comprehend older notions. In this light, we must look again at the documents of Vatican II. Isn't it clear that they are nothing but the unchanging doctrines of the Church specifically adapted for application within *individualistic, secularized, rights-based* societies.

In the past, when the Church was an institution intimately integrated into every level of social life, there was no danger of intolerance. The Church, in fact, was a bastion for religious freedom, despite the myths now spread about Inquisition and witch-hunts— convenient for secular states who are always trying to justify themselves. But Leo's prophecy about the implicit atheism of secularized governments had come to pass, and so the *emphasis* of the Church's message had to change along with the reality. A change in emphasis does not imply contradiction, but rather it displays its dynamism.

Because modern nations had become secular, man had to be protected *from the State* in his worship in a way that was never quite necessary before. The Church also had its own freedom threatened. This called for specific and new emphasis on religious liberty—hence the *Declaration on Religious Freedom*. Nothing was nullified, and what was declared in the past remained truth. Following the example of Christ, the Church preaches the truth, asks for perfection, but when man falls short, is always prepared to come minister to his wounds wherever he happens to be.

If we laid the entire collection of anti-Liberal documents right next to those produced during Vatican II—even *Dignitatis Humanae*—it is entirely possible to imagine that they were written by the same hand. All that we need in order to connect them and render their statements comprehensible is to imagine the following statement inserted between the two collections: "In the event that all of our warnings are ignored, and the worst should come to pass, see below:"

If every application of Church teachings "in the here and now" is contingent on present conditions, Vatican II was but the development and implementation of a new contingency plan.

n. Reception and Division

If we divided Catholics into groups based on their responses to the Council, we would come up with two: those who paid attention, and those who did not.

Of these, the second group comprises the vast majority of the laity. One of the unique aspects of the new era was that councils, synods, proclamations, declarations, exhortations, any other "official" actions of the Church ceased to matter to the man on the street. Just as the Church itself had been rendered as irrelevant to his daily routine, so also were the messages which issued from Her. Thus, the vast majority became insulated from the words of the Magisterium not by overt censorship but by the unconscious complacence that secularism instills. This left them to continue about their business without taking much notice of the whole affair.

But what of the other group?—those who were "waiting at the door" of the Council chamber, eager for its outcomes? These we can also divide again into two groups, based on whether their response was positive or negative. Yet that would not be sufficient, because on a very deep level both classes of reaction were evidence of a violent pessimism toward the Church Herself. What I mean is this:

Those who responded positively toward the new posture and plan of the Church, embracing the new emphasis of documents such as

Dignitatis Humanae seemed, in general, to believe that this marked a departure from previous teachings. They seemed to believe that the new contingency plan was not that at all, but was instead an admission of the Church's previous "backwardness" and that the Council had finally led the Church to "come around" to the truths of progress and Liberalism. And so this sort of response, although positive, is more accurately a sort of positive pessimism because it implies that the Church and its leaders, who worked so hard on behalf of man, had been laboring in vain all through the great war. It insinuated that the Church had been "on the wrong side of history."

Those who responded negatively to the outcomes of the Council held an opposite view which we can call "negatively pessimistic." They essentially agreed with the others that the Council represented not only a shift but a discontinuity in Church teachings. They only differed on which historical period they chose to reject: unlike their opponents, they sided with the warrior popes and rejected Vatican II, its participants, and its documents as heretical.

Neither of these two responses (whether a positive pessimism or a negative pessimism) seem to allow the possibility that it was not the doctor who changed but the patient. Neither seemed to be able (or perhaps, *willing?*) to give the Church the benefit of the doubt. The docility demanded by the Church is, it seems, one of its most difficult teachings.

And so, although there are no doubt many faithful Catholics who do not align with these general categories, the closing of the Council was met with two responses: indifference and pessimism. Coincidentally, both of these attitudes can be interpreted as symptoms of Liberalism, which can be expected to manifest itself differently according to the personality and disposition of each individual.

The Church is a prudent mother. She discerns when it is time to talk about something else. There is truth in the scriptural wisdom about throwing "pearls before swine." You aren't helping anyone by tossing them precious gems if their present condition prevents them from either appreciating or understanding the value of such things. The good shepherd feeds his flock—that was the mandate given to Peter. That is the task which concerns his successors. There may come a day when pearls—things of loftier value—are once again appropriate, but that is not today.

3. The Age of Ignorance

Let us tie all this together by observing the impact this process has had on knowledge in both its social and its individual aspects. We choose this subject because it is so often taken for granted that the modern world, if nothing else, has achieved wonderful things in the realm of knowledge.

If we had to summarize the frailty of man in one word, many of us would probably use the term "sin." Man is "fallen," we might respond. But to sin is simply *to miss the mark*. In what way does man tend to miss it?

To put the question differently, would it be more appropriate to describe fallen man as wicked, or could we say instead that he is merely stupid? Obviously both assertions are true: We all miss the mark quite frequently, both in thought and in behavior. But does the greater preponderance of our "woundedness" lie in our tendency toward immoral action, or, instead, in our innate ignorance?

Also, we should say that we do not mean to deal with these questions theologically, but rather sociologically: we don't want to talk about Aquinas's hierarchy of virtues; we want to talk about the way we perceive ourselves and those around us. And judging by the rhetoric we hear daily, it seems that most of us readily think of ourselves as morally frail, yet we become violently indignant when anyone suggests that we might, in addition, have vastly limited mental powers. This leads me to believe that somewhere along the line we chose the "wicked" answer and rejected almost completely the possibility that the greater problem was an epistemological one. We denied the possibility that, when Adam fell, he landed on his head.

It is the opinion of the Thomists and Antiquity that the preponderance of our human limitation can indeed be found in the intellectual sphere. Further, it seems that the conscious acknowledgment of this truth was the historical reality in traditional societies. Men of those times saw and accepted it with a humble realism, and they designed their sociopolitical framework accordingly.

At what point, then, did man's opinion about man begin to reverse itself? Undeniably this occurred alongside the rise of Liberalism we have been describing. With the victory of this movement, there came a massive shift in regard to how man views his own limited state, and we believe that this change represents one of the most profound upheavals in the history of the world.

We will begin with an observation from Erik von Kuehnelt-Leddihn, which states the case well:

> "In contradiction to St. Thomas (and to Luther, after all) the Church often seemed to take the position that *man is rather stupid than wicked*. Protestantism, though rather pessimistic about the spiritual qualities of the 'sin-cripple,' nevertheless gave him the Bible without explanatory footnotes, trusting in his intelligence (or 'inspiration'). Catholicism, on the other hand, frequently tended to adopt the view that a superficial half-education was much worse than no education at all, and thus in Catholic countries we saw (and

sometimes still see) a large number of illiterates side by side with an intellectual elite of high standards. The Protestant goal of education is usually one of *good averages*—the optimum for democracy. In democracies there will always be resentment and contempt for the 'highbrow' and the illiterate, the intellectual and the 'peasant.'"[63]

Through the Reformation this great shift in self-perception, by which man's carnal weakness and mental strength both became exaggerated, can be viewed with great clarity. Only within the context of this new, individualistic, rationalized, subjective sort of religiosity could the focus of hamartiology become so obsessed with man's "total depravity" while, at the very same time, laying on this same "totally depraved" soul the immense responsibility of interpreting scripture and discerning the truth of a thousand years of doctrine all by himself.

Yet we need to go further than just identifying historical transformations, which has been our project so far in this study. We need to examine the actual consequences of the change, the most significant of which, in the case of Liberalism, has been the unprecedented empowerment of ignorance as a social force.

As we've already seen, the situation shocked Tocqueville, who remarked that the political conditions in America bestowed on its people "a very lofty, often very exaggerated, conception of human reason." This, as we have shown, was the result of individualism fused with rationalism. If reason is a sufficient guide to truth, and every man is a self-sufficient island, then each man's reason is self-sufficient.

Thus, Americans came to entertain an incredible view of their individual intellectual competencies, and Tocqueville saw that it was

---

[63] *Liberty or Equality.*

democracy itself which presses this grandiose idea of one's own rationality onto the social psyche.

To understand this, consider the demands placed on the voting citizen. This "typical voter" requires two complex and very different areas of competence in order to assert himself honestly and effectively:

First, he must know the man for whom he is voting. If I do not know anything about you as a person, your strengths, weaknesses, experience, opinions, etc., then I am not competent to decide whether or not you can effectively govern, or do any other job for that matter. While I may conceivably achieve appropriate knowledge of this type about people who live down the street from me, it is nothing short of ludicrous to imagine that I can achieve that level of knowledge in regard to a presidential candidate whom I've never met and cannot meet, and about whom my only sources of information are a pair of warring tribes who either paint the candidate as a devil or a saint. The problems here are fairly obvious, but remember this is only the first area of competence I must achieve.

Second, after I attain knowledge of the candidate, I must attain knowledge of the job itself. If I do not know how the job works or what it is like, what strengths and aptitudes it requires, then I can't select someone to do the job even if I know all of the candidates personally.

Now here again, I can conceivably fulfill this second requirement of competence if the candidate in question lives down the street and will decide whether or not the forest across town gets cleared for development. I know the man, I know the forest, and I know the town. However, the knowledge required to truly know what it takes to be a "good president" is astonishingly complex: here one needs not only knowledge of history, geography, rhetoric, military science, international law, and foreign languages, but he also needs *experience*. If I have neither knowledge nor experience, then I'm like a baker trying to judge the technique of a brain surgeon: the baker might have an opinion on the surgeon's technique, but his opinion is not valid—it is but the expression of ignorance.

Because the attainment of the level of competence described above is obviously impossible for the average man who works and maybe even has a family, and because democracies like the United States are predicated on the notion that this same man can and should choose the president anyway, then democracy itself can be said to be predicated on the reinforcement of Augustinian ignorance. It not only suggests but *demands* that a man pick and choose between a thousand things he knows nothing about, and which he may have never even considered.

Needless to say, such an atmosphere is fertile ground for the enthronement of ignorance. Consider again our typical voting citizen:

1. He thinks he knows what's going on with global warming, whether the science is valid or not.

2. He thinks that he knows, at any given moment, what sort of effect a tax adjustment would have on the national economy.

3. He thinks he knows how immunizations work.

4. He thinks he knows what "organic" means.

5. He thinks he understands the conflict in the Middle East.

This list could go on and on, from Benghazi to the Big Bang, but I'm sure the point is clear: He cannot possibly have valid opinions about these things. Considered individually, the number of people who fully understand any one of the above points is undeniably very, very small. Considered as a whole and all at once, *no one could*

60

possibly have reached a level of understanding that could be termed "competent."

Further, although this alone is enough to achieve institutionalized solipsism, there is an even greater danger: it teaches men that *this is how truth is discovered*—by polling a mass of Augustinian opinionation and going with the greatest number.

This sort of "democratization of truth" ends by defeating itself. We think we have free thought, but it has been observed that never before was man more a slave to the opinions of others. To refer again to Tocqueville:

> "When conditions are unequal and men have dissimilar outlooks, there are a few very enlightened, learned, powerfully intelligent individuals while the masses are very ignorant and extremely limited. People who live under this aristocratic rule are naturally inclined to take as a guide for their opinions the superior reason of one man or one class, whereas they are not persuaded to recognize the infallibility of the masses.

> "In times of equality, the opposite prevails.

> "Gradually, as citizens become more equal and similar, the inclination for each man to have a blind belief in one particular man or class lessens. The predisposition to believe in mass opinion increases and becomes progressively the opinion which commands the world...

> "In the United States, the majority takes upon itself the task of supplying to the individual a mass of ready-made opinions, thus relieving him of the necessity to take the proper responsibility of arriving at his own."[64]

---

[64] *Democracy in America*, 2.1.2

This is why Thomas Jefferson himself lamented that "the inquisition of public opinion overwhelms, in practice, the freedom asserted by the law in theory." Odd sentiments for the Whig who penned the *Declaration of Independence*.

Even religious truth seemed to Tocqueville to have taken on this democratized guise: "Looking very closely, it can be seen that religion itself dominates less a revealed doctrine than a commonly held opinion." Religious truth ceases to be the result of authority (knowledge) and becomes instead a simple matter of *consensus*.

Yet the strangest aspect of this enthronement of ignorance, which would be ironic if it were not so sad, is that the philosophy of liberalism which is responsible for it receives, at one and the same time, universal devotion and burning hatred. The American party system, for example, is in reality nothing but a war between the right and left arms of the liberal leviathan. Both parties are liberal, but neither of them, due to ignorance of both history and logic, realize that the philosophy they hold is also the philosophy that they hate in the other tribe.

This was true even from the beginning. The great figures of the Reformation and the Enlightenment, though they may have at times hated each others' ideas, were merely applying the same ideas in different ways and in different fields. When Luther led liberalism against the church on one front, Voltaire did the same thing and with the same philosophy from an opposite front. Tocqueville is again our teacher:

> "The philosophers of the eighteenth century...undertook to expose to the personal scrutiny of each man the substance of all his beliefs. Who cannot see that Luther, Descartes, and Voltaire used the same method and that they differed from each other only in the greater and lesser use they claimed to make of it?"[65]

Men apparently so opposed were, in actuality, fighting on behalf of their enemy's philosophy. Liberalism, it seems, has a strange way of refusing to let those who hold it see it in its entirety. It reveals itself only in parts: one part to Luther, and another to Voltaire.

Things haven't changed much. Today in America we have "Right liberals and Left liberals," but everyone is a liberal. Our two parties are simply the Luthers (Republicans) fighting the Voltaires (Democrats)—the Pharisees against the Philistines. Historians will one day report, like Tocqueville, that they "differed from each other only in the greater and lesser use" they chose to make of their common philosophy.

Liberalism creates this chaos and this contradiction because they are its food and drink. It has a symbiotic relationship with strife. It takes one of its own adherents and gets that man to rant and rave against a "liberalism" which is nothing more than the other half of his own ideology. Thus, if liberalism were a religion, blasphemy would be one of its sacraments. In this way, liberalism always seems to be turning into its own opposite, promising Heaven and delivering shades of Hades.

Nor is liberalism truly liberating: Free speech is not free if what is said is not true. Thought is not free if it is not rational. Free opinion is a contradiction in terms if the opinion is an ignorant one. Thus liberalism, promising to deliver the individual from the arbitrary opinions of society, delivered him into total enslavement to the public. Public opinion now does not simply control man's body—it also forms his very mind and directs his will.

There are quite a few others who have noticed the disappearance of truly intelligent public discourse, and who have lamented the

---

65 Ibid.

63

shameless rise in assertive ignorance across the board. What no one seems to be able to explain, however, is the *why*.

That is the answer we've tried to provide, or at least approach, here. I've tried to illustrate that this endemic ignorance is not a new problem, or even a surprising one. It was seen from the beginning by perceptive observers. Tocqueville wrote hundreds of pages tracing it out

This is not the spontaneous breakout of a disease that we can simply endure, and least of all is it something we can cure with "more education." It is a system problem, and so long as the system persists it is unrealistic to expect people to behave in any other way.

It is time, then, to proceed to a vision of society that seeks to avoid these ills, and which we believe to be the most appropriate approach to social organization available to the Western World.

II. Foundations

Contained in this section are the basic principles on which the "Vision of the Structure" provided by the Church, is built.

1. Man

a. His Social Nature

The human person is called from the very beginning to lead a social life: "It is not good for man to be alone."[66] This is why the Church teaches that "God did not create man as a 'solitary being' but wished him to be a 'social being'. Social life therefore is not exterior to man: he can only grow and realize his vocation in relation with others."[67]

And again:

> "Men, families and the various groups which make up the civil community are aware that they cannot achieve a truly human life by their own unaided efforts. They see the need for a wider community, within which each one makes his specific contribution every day toward an ever broader realization of the common good. For this purpose they set up a political community according to various forms. The political community exists, consequently, for the sake of the common good, in which it finds its full justification and significance, and the source of its inherent legitimacy. Indeed, the common good embraces the sum of those conditions of the social life whereby men, families and associations more adequately and readily may attain their own perfection."[68]

---

[66] *Gen* 2:18.
[67] *LC,* 32.
[68] *Gaudium et Spes,* 74.

Being made in the image and likeness of the triune God, the human person is naturally communal and distinguished from other creatures in this respect. The Church proclaims this truth about man constantly, and all of Catholic Social Teaching presupposes it.[69] Even in addressing issues of a purely economic concern, the need for communion is kept central. As Benedict XVI stated:

> "One of the deepest forms of poverty a person can experience is isolation. If we look closely at other kinds of poverty, including material forms, we see that they are born from isolation, from not being loved or from difficulties in being able to love."[70]

b. The Enlightenment and the "Social Contract"

This leaves little room for the so-called "libertarian" mentality, which would conceive of man as a "noble savage" who enters into society only as a necessary evil rather than as a natural good. Such a view, although it seems quite normal today, is quite modern and is in fact a product of Enlightenment humanism. Only during that period did it become a core doctrine, eventually evolving into the school of thought known as Liberalism. If, taking a wider view, we survey human history in general, we find that this anti-social point of view is quite in the minority. If we survey Christian history specifically, we find that it is non-existent.

c. Personal Development

We are warned never to lose sight of the interdependence of man and his fellows. "The human person may never be thought of only as an absolute individual being, built up by himself and on himself."[71]

---

[69] See also: *GS*, 12; *CCC*, 1879; *PT*, 23; *LP*, 10.

[70] *CV*, 53.

[71] *CSDC*, 125.

If we are to consider personal growth and realization in its fullness, we must be able to acknowledge the role of personal responsibility in the development of the individual, while at the same time taking into account our profound need for community. Pope Benedict XVI elaborated on the paradox:

> "The human person by nature is actively involved in his own development...since as everybody knows, we are all capable of making free and responsible choices. Nor is it merely at the mercy of our caprice, since we all know that we are a gift, not something self-generated. Our freedom is profoundly shaped by our being, and by its limits. No one shapes his own conscience arbitrarily, but we all build our own 'I' on the basis of a 'self' which is given to us. Not only are other persons outside our control, but each one of us is outside his or her own control. A person's development is compromised, if he claims to be solely responsible for producing what he becomes."[72]

d. Social Sin

Although the Church does not spend a great deal of time developing the theological understanding of sin, it necessarily takes it into account as it pertains to the subject. What this means is that Catholic Social Teaching acknowledges not only the personal aspect of sin, but also its social aspect. It teaches that "every sin is social insofar as and because it also has social consequences."[73] While sin is a result of the personal actions of an individual's free will, yet by virtue of human solidarity every sin of the individual directly impacts his neighbor. This is not by any means an attempt to cancel the responsibility of the individual sinner, but is rather, as was

---

[72] *CV,* 68.
[73] *CSDC,* 117.

suggested above, an examination of sinfulness from its interpersonal aspect, which complements its individual aspect.

e. The Law of Descent—the Law of Ascent

To express the same thing in terms used by St. John Paul II, we can say that as a consequence of the social aspect of sin it is appropriate to speak of a "law of descent" which is a kind of "communion of sin" by which each sinful soul drags down the whole Church along with it. On the bright side, this also implies a corresponding "law of ascent" which operates by virtue of the "communion of saints," and so it is said that "every soul that rises above itself, raises up the world."[74]

The body of Christ is a unity that hangs together, for better or worse, in solidarity unto the end. It is precisely this social reality which informs the Catholic principle of solidarity which we will discuss below. For if our lives are intertwined, and if it is easier to live virtuously when material conditions are at an optimum level, then we ought to do our utmost to lift our neighbors from want, and we ought to see clearly that our own prosperity is not enough.

f. Rights and Duties

We proceed next to the notion of "right," and this for two reasons. First, because it is a word that is on the tip of every tongue these days and so it seems reasonable to address the most familiar and pressing issues first. This will allow us to iron out any misconceptions that may exist, and clear the way for other issues that may have been obscured by the confusion. Second, we address the issue of right because it is directly linked to man's social nature, which is to say: *rights are social.*

---

[74] *RP*, 16.

Specific applications will be avoided at this point in favor of a few general observations about the nature of the right. For example, we will forgo the discussion of individual rights (such as those pertaining to life, speech, worship, etc.) until they present themselves naturally in the course of our study.

g. Rights Imply Relation

St. Thomas Aquinas said that "right is the object of justice."[75] It is here that we can see the social or *relational* aspect of the right, since justice implies two parties. Insofar as a man is bound by justice, he is bound in a relationship, even if we reduce this relationship to its most primordial level, such as the original relation between creature and Creator. What follows from this observation is that there is really no such thing as a purely "individual" right which one claims for oneself against the claims of others and which is owed to him absolutely without distinction and unconditionally. Just as there are two parties in the relationship, there are two aspects of justice, and the right is only one of them—the other aspect being *duty*. If duty is neglected, the concept of right is undermined from the start. Nicholas Gomez-Davila struck at the heart of this confusion when he lamented: "It has become customary to proclaim rights in order to be able to violate duties."[76] To violate one's own duty is automatically to violate the rights of another.

h. Rights Presuppose Duties

The Catholic Church always addresses the notion of right and duty at the same time. The former cannot be separated from the latter without undermining both. Following the reasoning of St. John XXIII, we can say that rights "are inextricably bound up with as many duties, all applying to one and the same person. These rights

---

[75] *ST* II-II, q. 57, a. 1.

[76] *Scholia to an Implicit Text*, 2587.

and duties derive their origin, their sustenance, and their indestructibility from the natural law, which in conferring the one imposes the other."[77] To use but one example, we can say that the right to life carries with it the duty to preserve one's life. The two components are two sides of the same coin: "to claim one's rights and ignore one's duties, or only half fulfill them, is like building a house with one hand and tearing it down with the other."[78] This is why the Church, sensing an unfortunate "gap" between the *letter* and the *spirit* of rights,[79] calls for the constant fostering of a social sense that remains aware of the needs of the common good.[80]

i. Rights are not Absolute

From this we can surmise that rights are not to be considered absolute. The Church calls them "inalienable," which is to say, they are derived from human nature, but their *exercise* must always be circumscribed within limits. They are "contingent." To take but one common example, the Church has consistently proclaimed the right to private property, and yet the *Compendium* says plainly that "*Christian tradition has never recognized the right to private property as absolute and untouchable.*"[81] It will be appropriate to elaborate further on this particular point when we arrive at our discussion of private property below. For now, we need only illustrate that the notion of "right" is a balance, and is just as much directed outward, toward neighbor, as it is inward, toward the self. Rights must never become captive to a self-centered, egoistic paradigm if they are to remain healthy and functional.

---

[77] *PT*, 28.
[78] *PT*, 30.
[79] *RH*, 17.
[80] *OA*, 23.
[81] *CSDC*, 177.

2. Society

a. The Family as the Basic Unit of Society

Perhaps the greatest difference between the Catholic and Liberal view of politics is that for the Catholic the cell of the social body is the family, and not the individual.

Just as God is a Trinity, and cannot be considered as three separate Gods each going separate ways, so the fundamental social unit is the family, and not the individual as father, mother or child.[82] The family is the basic unit of political and economic organization in the Catholic tradition. As an association, it is prior to every other. "It is in this cradle of life and love that people are born and grow."[83] Here the person takes his first steps into his personhood, learns responsibility, and develops his manifold potentialities. The family is the "fundamental structure for human ecology."[84]

Because man is fundamentally a social being, it can be said that "only insofar as he understands himself in reference to a 'thou' can he say 'I'." It is in the family that he "comes out of himself, from the self-centered preservation of his own life, to enter into a relationship of dialogue and communion with others."[85] This is why no law can threaten this institution—the State exists for the family and not the family for the State.

> "No human law can abolish the natural and original right of marriage, nor in any way limit the chief and original purpose of marriage, ordained by God's authority from the beginning. Increase and multiply. Hence we have the Family; the 'society' of a man's house—a society limited

---

[82] *LS*, 157.

[83] *CSDC*, 212.

[84] *CA*, 39.

[85] *CSDC*, 130; See also: *LS*, 213.

indeed in numbers, but no less a true society, anterior to every kind of State or Nation, invested with rights and duties of its own, totally independent of the civil community...Inasmuch as the domestic household is antecedent, as well in idea as in fact, to the gathering of men into a community, the Family must necessarily have rights and duties which are prior to those of the community, and founded more immediately in nature...The contention then, that the civil government should at its option intrude into and exercise intimate control over the Family and the household, is a great and pernicious error."[86]

Pius XI affirmed this teaching in *Casti Connubii*, referring to marriage as "the principle and foundation of domestic society, and therefore of all human intercourse."[87]

b. The Purpose of Society and the State

James Madison famously said that "if men were angels, no government would be necessary." This statement is as false as it is ignorant, because nearly every reputable theologian since Augustine has maintained that the angels are in fact governed, and that they are governed absolutely. In fact, the only angels that are not governed are in Hell. However, it is easy to see that it was not theology but political prejudice which led Madison into his error, because Enlightenment Liberalism tended always to view society as something unnatural to man—something against his nature and which was only accepted as a compromise or a "necessary evil."

In the Catholic view, as we have already observed, social life is a gift and government is a divinely instituted good. Solomon says that "Where there is no governor, the people shall fall."[88] And Paul

---

[86] *RN*, 12-14.
[87] *CC*, 1.

warns that there is no authority except that which God has established.[89] Yet it is also true that the State exists for man, and not man for the State.[90] God established authority, but for man and not for itself.

If we apply the principles of solidarity and subsidiarity, we can sum up the purpose of the State by saying that it is to serve the common good by fulfilling those requirements which cannot be met by lower associations. These can be roughly enumerated as keeping the peace between lower social bodies, providing for defense from foreign invaders, and seeing to the maintenance of distributive justice. In a healthy society the role of the State need not be extensive or overly intrusive. The State is, however, completely necessary. Only in society can man fulfill himself, and this means that political life is part of his nature. Social and political activities are justified in their existence because of man, and should not be viewed as something erected over and against him.

It does not follow from this that the government which governs least, governs best.[91] The opposite may just as often prove true. The State has a distinct role to play, and it must be judged, not based on how much or little it governs, but by whether or not it carries out the functions proper to it. It "exists to achieve an end otherwise unobtainable: the full growth of each of its members, called to cooperate steadfastly for the attainment of the common good, under the impulse of their natural inclinations towards what is true and good."[92]

---

[88] *Eccl* 4:9.
[89] *Rom* 13:1.
[90] *CCC*, 1881; *GS*, 25.
[91] *Economic Justice for All*, 124.
[92] *CSDC*, 384.

c. *The End of the State is the End of Man*

Because the State exists to assist man in realizing the potentialities of his nature, and because his vocation is in its noblest sense a spiritual one, then political society fails automatically if it does not take into consideration anything more than the temporal lives of its citizens.[93] As it has been put by Aquinas:

> "[T]he same judgment is to be formed about the end of society as a whole as about the end of one man...If such an ultimate end either of an individual man or a multitude were a corporeal one, namely, life and health of body, to govern would then be a physician's charge. If that ultimate end were an abundance of wealth, then knowledge of economics would have the last word in the community's government. If the good of the knowledge of truth were of such a kind that the multitude might attain to it, the king would have to be a teacher. It is, however, clear that the end of a multitude gathered together is to live virtuously. For men form a group for the purpose of *living well* together, a thing which the individual man living alone could not attain, and *good life* is virtuous life. Therefore, virtuous life is the end for which men gather together...Yet through virtuous living man is further ordained to a higher end, which consists in the enjoyment of God...Consequently, since society must have the same end as the individual man, it is not the ultimate end of an assembled multitude to live virtuously, but through virtuous living to attain to the possession of God."[94]

Now these words should not be interpreted as a demand for State-run churches, mandatory attendance of the mass, and the like. Aquinas is merely acknowledging the fact that the State, since it

---

[93] *CSDC*, 386.
[94] *DR*, 106-107.

plays the governing role in society, cannot make pretenses at spiritual indifference. Let it try to adopt the stance of indifferentism, and it will end by establishing a practical atheism.

So what might Aquinas's vision look like in practice? To take but one example, the Church calls on the State to ensure that workers have a sufficient amount of rest, not merely to repair the strain placed on the body during labor, but so that workers can properly devote themselves to their spiritual exercises which can easily fall into neglect. Man must therefore be provided with rest for both soul and body, and not for the body alone.[95] By such simple measures we can see how the State ought to act in favor of the religious life without assuming responsibility for it.

3. Law

Now we must proceed to law itself, which is today a very convoluted subject. Under democratic regimes, for example, the law tends to be whatever the people wish it to be, or else whatever the lawmakers find expedient at the time. The only standard for legislation is that it pass a vote. This means that law has no objective content whatsoever.

In the Catholic view, law is derived from above, and it is the function of lawmakers to "realize the law," not to "make" it. They are to apply a standard that exists independent of either the will of the people or the agendas of the lobbyists.

This law is most often discussed under the aspect of "natural law," which is appropriate. However, we need to understand exactly what this law is and how its contents are discerned.

---

[95] *RN*, 41-42.

a. Which law? What nature?

Whenever someone mentions "natural law" there is an immediate confusion that usually arises due to the contemporary understanding of the word "nature." In modern usage we associate the terms "nature" and "natural" with the "natural world," which is to say, the universal laws of physics and biology and all of the mechanisms that take place on this level. We don't attribute to the word "nature" anything specifically human. It is taken as a context for all life rather than as a distinctive characteristic of a given being.

But when the Church speaks of "nature," and especially when it speaks of natural law, it is speaking very differently. This is because natural law teaches that every being has its own "nature," and that this imbedded nature also corresponds to an imbedded "natural law" which tends the being toward the perfection of its specific nature. It follows then that the "nature" in question will always be different depending on whether we are talking about a vegetable, an animal, or the human person. What is according to the "natural law" for one category of beings may not apply to another, because they have different natures. This is why the tendency to imagine "nature" as mere biological necessity applying to all material beings *in the same way* is a drastic oversimplification. Rather, when we are concerned with human behavior, we are concerned with man's specific nature and, more importantly, his last end toward which this nature tends to move.

For example, we might say that sexual desire is "natural." If we make the mistake of taking "natural law" to mean "biological necessity," then we might end up drawing the conclusion that promiscuous sex is according to the natural law, since we see it all the time in animals and in fact this behavior is necessary to many of them. But we cannot transpose this principle onto a different nature—for example, onto human nature. Sexual desire is still in accordance with natural law for human nature, but only insofar as it reinforces the being's development toward its ultimate perfection. While for certain animal natures this entails promiscuous sex, for man it does not. Sexual desire is therefore "natural" to man in a very different way than it is "natural" to animals, because man has different faculties and a different perfection which he must realize. He *has a different nature* and so the natural law does not direct him in the same way as it would direct a vegetable; likewise, the vegetable is directed very differently than a fish or a bird.

In order to gain a proper perspective on this subject, we must return to a more comprehensive notion of law capable of taking into account a hierarchy of orders and contexts, and which can deal with the diversity of life we find in the world. In traditional terminology, we must return to the three orders of law: eternal, natural, human.

b. Eternal law

Whenever we come upon a community of beings ruled by a sovereign who directs them toward their good, we come upon a law. If there are different kinds of these communities, they will be directed by a different kind of law. Now, the first and foremost of communities is the universe. The universe and every being within it are sustained in their very existence by the will of God and act in accordance with his rule. From this single rule, which is called *eternal law*, all other varieties of law are derived.[96]

c. Natural law

In every created thing there is an inclination, impressed upon the very substance of the creature, drawing it toward certain ends. These ends are the mark of what the *eternal law* demands of that specific nature. It follows logically that this law will be different for

---

[96] *ST* I-II, q. 91, a. 1; *ST* I-II, q. 93, aa. 1-6.

each nature, depending on the *end* toward which the eternal law directs it. Man, for example, has divine beatitude for his end, whereas animals and vegetable life do not. And so, the inclinations of each will vary. When we obey this law which is "written on our natures,"[97] we obey the law of our nature—our *natural law*. Because this natural law is really just the eternal as it pertains to us as men, then it is true that when we obey it we are participating in the eternal law. This is why it is said that the natural law is derived from and never contradicts the eternal law.[98]

d. Human law

Why then, if there is a natural law written in the hearts of men, do we not find the same laws and customs in every society? Why, if all men possess the same nature and therefore the same natural law, does every society have different laws? The explanation for this lies in the third kind of law, which is called *human law*. The difference between natural law and human law is that natural law provides general precepts which are everywhere the same, while human law represents particular applications of these precepts. Because every nation and historical period differs and therefore has different needs, its *applications* of the precepts will be incredibly diverse, even though the precepts themselves will remain the same. This is a valid diversity so long as they accord with natural law and, through this, eternal law. It is only by ultimately deriving from the eternal law that any lower form of law has its validity:

> "Human law is law only by virtue of its accordance with right reason; and thus it is manifest that it flows from the eternal law. And in so far as it deviates from right reason it is called an unjust law; in such case it is no law at all, but rather a species of violence."[99]

---

[97] *ST* I-II, q. 94, a. 6.
[98] *ST* I-II, q. 91, a. 2.

e. The precepts of the natural law

In order to understand why human law is diverse while natural law is said to be everywhere the same, we must remember that, much as the Church offers principles rather than technical solutions, the natural law offers *precepts* rather than applications. And the first precept of the natural law is simply this: *good is to be sought and evil avoided.*[100]

Further precepts are dictated by man's nature: he is a being, he is a living being, and he is a rational being. Corresponding to these three facts about man's nature are three natural precepts: first, man must conserve his being, which we call the duty of "self-preservation"; further, he must reproduce himself, raise his children, etc.; and last, which is specific to man as a rational being, he is to actively seek what is good. It is only due to this last feature that man can be considered "responsible" for his decisions. Animals, being irrational and therefore unable to rationally seek conformity with the natural law, follow it automatically and without their conscious assent. Only man can consciously participate in, or revolt against, the natural law.

From these observations we can begin to see why human law is diverse. Although the precepts are everywhere the same, we should expect that, depending on time and place, people will find various means of fulfilling these precepts. Also, because some of these men will make better use of their rational faculties, the various human laws will be more or less in conformity to the natural law. All will not be equal, although all can be said to be striving after the same justice.

---

[99] *ST* I-II, q. 93, a. 3.
[100] *ST* I-II, q. 94, a. 2.

f. Not everything in nature is natural

One further confusion needs to be set aright, if only because it is so common. Consider the following statement: "Whatever exists, is found in nature, and is therefore natural." This way of thinking—called "naturalism"—leads to the rejection of any morality whatsoever, because it rejects the possibility of anything being unnatural. But we must recall that the Church does not speak of "nature" simply in terms of "everything that exists." Certainly the Church acknowledges the totality of creation as "nature," but it considers it as a grand diversity and within the context of natural law, which takes into account the particular *end* toward which a being tends. Considered in this way, if an action or behavior conforms with its proper end (or its "perfection"),[101] then and only then is it natural. Thus, we can easily imagine acts which are in no way ordained to the proper end of the nature in question. For example, the sexual function and the pleasure associated with it are natural insofar as they conform to their obvious natural ends; they are unnatural when they do not. The deviant who seeks pleasure with himself alone short-circuits both the purpose of the sexual function and the pleasure associated with it. An analogous consideration can be found in the intellectual sphere: although human reasoning is performed by the "rational faculty," no one would be naïve enough to claim that every decision produced by this faculty is therefore rational. Whether or not a decision is rational depends not on whether or not it is produced through the rational faculty, but whether or not it was produced in conformity with the laws proper to that sphere. It is entirely possible for the rational faculty to produce irrational conclusions. Returning now to the sphere of natural law, we must not lose our ability to distinguish the normal ("natural") from the pathological ("unnatural"), simply because they both appear "in nature."

---

[101] *ST* I-II, q. 94, a. 2.

4. The Good

The Catholic also believes that men legitimately pursue "happiness," but he does not allow, as do the Liberals, that this happiness is some subjective term that the individual is free to fill with whatever content he wishes. For the Catholic, happiness lies in the "good life." But what is the good life? Or, what must be answered first, what is "the good?"

a. Definition

The good is what all men desire. If anyone desires an evil, it is only because it appears to him to be good. Goods can be divided into three categories: pleasant (a ham sandwich), useful (money), and honorable (friendship).

Because we find ourselves in the physical world, our knowledge begins with the senses. This leads us to desire first of all goods which please the senses such as food and water. These *pleasant* goods we also call *sensible.*

As we develop in understanding we come to desire not just the food, but also the means of obtaining the food, such as money. We expand our desire to *useful* goods.

As we develop to our highest potential, we begin to desire and obtain the *honorable* goods—knowledge, beauty, truth, love, etc.— and these in proportion to our progress in knowledge.

b. The Good is a Final Cause

The end or purpose for which a thing acts is called its final cause. All beings, as we said, act for the good. Thus, the good is a final cause. And since this final cause is desired by all things, we can say that it is *the* final cause. It is the cause of all causes. It is "the beginning and the end," the Alpha and the Omega. The good, then, is God, and God is the absolute good for which all things act.

c. Private Good

Sensible goods like the ham sandwich are called *private* because they can only be the good of one person at a time. They are, in a manner of speaking, limited and ordered to the user.

By their nature, private goods cannot be shared without being diminished. If you eat a particular sandwich, then it follows that I cannot also eat that sandwich.

To love a private good is not to love that particular good but to love the one whose good it is. To love a sandwich and give it away is to love the person to whom I have given it. To the extent that we love our own private goods, we love ourselves.

d. Common Good

Goods are called *common* when they can be shared without being diminished. Friendship is a common good because I lose nothing when I share it with a comrade. In fact, it is obvious that a good such as friendship cannot exist in any other way than as a shared good. If it were not shared, it would not exist.

Here we must state emphatically that a true common good is not a collection of private goods. It is not a whole made by the sum of so many parts. It resists quantification and is thus a *supra-individual* good. It differs from the private good not in quantity, but in quality.

e. Common Good is Superior to Private Good

According to St. Thomas Aquinas, a cause is greater as it extends its causality to more effects. If this is true, then the common good exceeds the private good:

"For it is manifest that any cause is the more powerful inasmuch as it extends itself to more effects. Whence also the good, which has the notion of a final cause, is the more powerful inasmuch as it extends itself to more things. And therefore, if the same thing is the good of one man and of the whole city, it seems much better and more perfect to undertake - that is, to procure, to defend and to preserve - that which is the good of the whole city than that which is the good of one man. For it pertains to the love which ought to exist among men that a man seek and conserve the good even of only one man, but it is much better and more divine that this be shown to the whole people and to the cities."[102]

f. Preference for the Private Good is Disordered

When I prefer a private good to a common good, my love is disordered. Note that I have not said that a person may not love his private good—only that he may not subordinate a common good to it.

For example, we have all had the experience of losing an argument. In such a situation, we often continue to argue our case beyond the point at which we realize we are wrong. For the sake of a private good (our self-esteem) we are willing to sacrifice a common good (truth and knowledge). When we let go of the former to accept the latter, our love falls back into proper order. We are not required to stop loving ourselves, because self-love is not only healthy but is in fact a duty. On the contrary, we are simply required to keep our loves in their proper order by giving precedence to the truth.

---

[102] *In Ethic.* I, lect. 2.

g. Personal Dignity

We say that man is a person made in the image of God, and that from this he derives his dignity. But what does this really mean? It means, first of all, that man's dignity is a matter of *participation*. He possesses dignity because he participates in a good that is clearly higher than himself. Because the extent to which he participates in higher goods exceeds that of all other earthly beings, we are right in considering him exceptional—that is to say more dignified than the rest.

For example, a stone exists, and so has some manner of dignity because it participates in existence; a plant lives, and so it has a higher dignity than the rock by participation in life; the beast exists, lives, and obtains to sentience, and so has the highest dignity yet. But then there is man, who exists, feels, and *thinks*. Man is rational, and in this capacity he is the apex of creation. Man is therefore the master of creation because he represents the highest degree of participation in God's goodness.

An important point is that his dignity is found by reference to a higher being. Man's dignity is therefore relational, discovered through reference to a higher being. Man is not the measure of himself, much less is he the "measure of all things."

h. Personal Dignity is Rooted in the Common Good

Because dignity is obtained to the degree that a being participates in higher goods, and because man participates in goods of varying degrees, both private and common, it behooves us to ask which of these—private or common—is the root of that personal dignity which makes him master among earthly creatures?

The answer follows from what has already been said. If the common good is higher than the private, then man's dignity should be rooted in the common rather than the private order. To object to this point by saying that man's dignity derives directly from God is really no objection at all, for God is the Supreme Common Good.

i. God is the Supreme Common Good

God, in his plenitude, is communicable to all beings at one and the same time without being diminished thereby. This is the definition of a common good. God is thus the supreme Common Good. Furthermore, we should recall that in order to have a common good we must share it. This is most true of God. If we wish to enjoy Him, we must share Him, and if we will not share Him, we may not have Him, for He cannot be reduced to the status of private good.

To quote Professor Ralph McInerny:

> "It is not the Catholic view that human persons relate to God one-to-one, so to speak, with God being *my* good in an exclusive sense. Indeed, to love God merely as to *my* good would be a defective love. It would be to turn God into my private good, as if there were commensurability between my finite will and infinite goodness. The only appropriate way to love God is as a good infinitely shareable. The rule of charity makes this clear. I must love my neighbor as, like myself, ordered to a common good."[103]

j. Liberalism and Social Disorder

At this point we may answer an objection that goes something like this: The common good of society has as its end the material well-being of man, while man has as his end eternal beatitude. Eternal beatitude is higher than material well-being, and so the private good is higher than the common.

---

[103] Ralph McInerny, *Art and Prudence*, Ch. 6.

85

This argument is false on a variety of levels. First we can say that eternal beatitude is not a private good—that just because each person is called to it does not mean that it is not common. Second, it misunderstands the end of human society, which is the same as the end of man. Both terminate in the vision of God. The common good and the private good are, therefore, ordered to the same lofty end.

If we are unable to imagine the private and the common sharing the same end, it is only because we have become inundated with secular liberalism which sought to reduce the purpose of society to exclusively worldly concerns while relegating eternal concerns to the private sphere. Only by assuming the presence of a disordered social life does the argument above hold true.

k. The Private Good is Realized in the Common Good

Having observed that God is the absolute common good, and that the end of the human person is perfection in God; and having observed that the common good is higher—more perfect—than the private good, we can say that the end of man depends for its fullest realization on participation in the common good. The common good does not nullify the private good but elevates it and brings it to a fruition which it could never have achieved in its own sphere.

As an example, consider a basketball team whose end is victory. This end is shared by all members of the team. It is in this way an end belonging to each one of them individually. But if any individual attempts to appropriate that end as a private good he will never achieve it. If victory is to be enjoyed, it must be enjoyed in common by all, because it is a common good.

All goods share an end. If they appear separate—as is the case with private and common—it is not because they are in opposition but because they belong to separate orders. They are two rungs on the same ladder leading to Heaven. Both are necessary, but one is higher.

1. Political Society is not the Common Good

At this point we might answer a second objection, usually proffered by quoting the following statement from Pope Pius XI: *Society is for man and not vice versa!*

True indeed, and this does seem to subordinate society to man. But let us look at the context of the statement:

> "In the plan of the Creator, society is a natural means which man can and must use to reach his destined end. Society is for man and not vice versa. This must not be understood in the sense of liberalistic individualism, which subordinates society to the selfish use of the individual; but only in the sense that by means of an organic union with society and by mutual collaboration the attainment of earthly happiness is placed within the reach of all. In a further sense, it is society which affords the opportunities for the development of all the individual and social gifts bestowed on human nature. These natural gifts have a value surpassing the immediate interests of the moment, for in society they reflect the divine perfection, which would not be true were man to live alone."[104]

The conclusion is simply this: *Political society is not the common good, but a necessary means of facilitating man's participation in it.* In this light, it is perfectly reasonable to say that man is ordered to the common good, and yet at the same time declare that society is for man, and not man for society. Society is for man, that he may achieve a full participation in the common good.

---

[104] *Divini Redemptoris*, 29

Finally, we answer a third objection. Under the influence of economic liberalism, it has become common to say that individualism (preference for the private good) is not only permissible but is in fact beneficial, since the collective action of selfish individuals will, in the long run, benefit the society as a whole. Thus, man helps his fellows best when he attends only to himself. No conscious preference for the common good is necessary, and in fact it is harmful and short-circuits the system, which runs most productively on self-interest.

Now, even if we granted the accuracy of such a premise—that economies run best on self-interest—it would not vindicate such a system or render it good for man, whether privately or in common. This is because the love for the common good cannot occur *accidentally* or unintentionally as a bi-product of selfish efforts. The common good must be sought—and that is to say *loved*—for what it is:

> "Now one can love the good of a city in two ways: in one way to possess it, in another that it might be preserved. If someone loves the good of a city in order to have and own it, he is not a good political person, because in this way even a tyrant loves the good of a city, in order to dominate it, which is to love oneself more than the city. He wants this good for himself, not for the city...But to love that good according to itself, that it may remain and be shared out and that nothing be done against this good, this gives to a person the right relation to that society of the blessed. And this is love [*caritas*] which loves God for his sake and the neighbors, who are capable of blessedness, as oneself."[105]

---

[105] *De Virtutibus*, 2.2c.

To operate on the liberal premise, according to Aquinas, is to make of each man a tyrant.[106]

n. Summary

To summarize and close this subject we can refer to Fr. Sebastian Walshe, from whose dissertation the author has drawn great benefit:

> "Dignity for the created person implies participation in an order more perfect than his own being. The human person ascends from being to the ultimate common good through the intermediate common goods of society and the natural order. Without a love for each of these orders and a right appreciation for these orders which is presupposed to this love the human person cannot attain to the ultimate good which is the whole source of his personal dignity. When a person treats these goods as a means to his private good, instead of as ends more lovable in themselves than his private good, the order of love is perverted. Man constructs an order of goods which is nothing more than a turning inward upon his own being for the sake of his own existence. In this order all things are ultimately ordained to the preservation of the body and bodily pleasure so that the goods of this perverted order become successively more contracted and imperfect. In the place of the ladder of Jacob the tower of Babel is raised."[107]

---

[106] *De Regno,* ch. 1.
[107] Fr. Sebastian Walshe, *The Primacy of the Common Good as the Root of Personal Dignity,* p. 334.

5. The Authority of the Church

a. The Origin of Authority

Having outlined above our position in history, acknowledging also the preconceptions and prejudices which go to form our unique mentality, we may proceed to one of the aspects of the orientation we are proposing for the American Catholic. We begin at the most logical starting point, by identifying the source of all social authority.

On this point, we need not limit ourselves to Catholic teachings in particular, because all traditional civilizations have been unanimous: *There is no authority except that which God has established: The authorities that exist have been established by God.*[108] Whether we are speaking of the Egyptians or the Hebrews who were their slaves; whether the Chinese in the Far East or the Hindus in India, the genesis of the social order is in Heaven. All power descended from this transcendent pivot: first to whatever priestly caste there happened to be, and then to the royalty whose role was governance and war, and then continuing through the social hierarchy depending on function.

We are the first great civilization to deny this principle. Liberalism taught the inverse of the old paradigm: that authority does not descend from the Heavens but rather *ascends* from the consent of the governed. This is one of the defining features of our time, not in the sense that older societies did not depend on the "consent of the governed," for in reality all governments at all times have depended on that. But what distinguishes us is that we insist on this as the

---

[108] *Romans* 13:1.

efficient cause, and not just a *material cause,* of all legitimate social authority.

We need not elaborate this point in detail now, but must only acknowledge it in passing so that when St. Thomas Aquinas says that "those to whom pertains the care of intermediate ends should be subject to him to whom pertains the care of the ultimate end, and be directed by his rule...Consequently, in the law of Christ, kings must be subject to priests,"[109] then we may know that he meant it.

b. Body and Soul

Another image frequently used to designate the role of the Church in society is that of *body* and *soul.* While Paul's *Epistle to the Romans* emphasizes hierarchy, the analogy of body and soul emphasizes complementarity, while still retaining Paul's hierarchical implications, because the soul governs the body, being its *form.*[110]

This was the imagery adopted by Leo XIII in *Immortale Dei,* when speaking on this subject:

> "There must, accordingly, exist between these two powers a certain orderly connection, which may be compared to the union of the soul and body in man. The nature and scope of that connection can be determined only, as We have laid down, by having regard to the nature of each power, and by taking account of the relative excellence and nobleness of their purpose. One of the two has for its proximate and chief object the well-being of this mortal life; the other, the everlasting joys of heaven."[111]

---

[109] *De Regno,* 110.
[110] Aquinas says that "by the virtue of the soul the body is formed, and then the latter is governed and moved by the soul" (*De Regno,* 97). And again: "in the individual man, the soul rules the body" (*De Regno,* 9).
[111] *Immortale Dei,* 14.

This division of rule between two powers, each corresponding to its own sphere, is the same *Gelasian dyarchy* we have already mention, citing the famous letter of Pope Gelasius I to Emperor Anastasius.

Aquinas uses the same analogy to describe a relation of lower rank: that between a prince and his people: "Therefore let the king recognize that such is the office which he undertakes, namely, that he is to be in the kingdom what the soul is in the body, and what God is in the world."[112] This does not invalidate the previous application of the analogy to Church and State; Aquinas is merely applying the analogy to a different relation, and he continues to do so on down the hierarchy to the level of the individual person and his inner relations.

c. Spiritual Authority and Temporal Power

The priority of the Church cannot be understood apart from the relationship between "spiritual authority" and "temporal power." Or, said another way, between knowledge and action. A look at this relationship show us that what has been said above was not some arbitrary mandate of the almighty, but was a logical necessity that could not be any other way. *Knowledge must always precede action* in order to be considered free, rational, and human. Action not informed by knowledge can only be instinctual and animal.

Because the priestly caste is always concerned with the spiritual principles which go to form the basis of all other knowledge, and because they are nearest to God who is the source of all truth, all other forms of knowledge emanate from the one maintained and cultivated by them. All other sciences are subordinate to the Divine Science. It was on this principle, and not on superstition and primitive fear, that all traditional hierarchies were constructed. What is Justice, Mercy, Truth, and the nature of the human person?

---

[112] *De Regno*, 95.

Whether we are speaking of a prince, a president, or Pontius Pilate,[113] the proper exercise of temporal power is impossible without first seeking the answers to these questions; and they are questions only a spiritual authority can answer.

In order to convey this perennial truth, a variety of symbols and illustrations have been used. Consider Aesop's fable of the lame man and the blind man. The blind man represents *action* or temporal power, for he has physical strength but lacks the guiding light of "vision." The lame man, on the other hand, represents *knowledge* because, while enlightened by "vision," he is materially weak. In the fable, the blind man carries the lame man on his back, who watches and guides his steps. The relationship is simultaneously cooperative and hierarchical. They both benefit, but the "sight" of knowledge *must come before* each movement if the precipice is to be avoided.

Another example appears in that legendary relationship between Merlin, the Druid, and King Arthur. St. Thomas even goes so far as to identify the hierarchical superiority of the Druidic priests as a prefiguration of the relationship between the clergy and Christian princes of the Middle Ages.[114]

d. Spheres of Competence

It has been mentioned already, but it must be emphasized again that the Church and the State do indeed have their own proper spheres in which they are largely autonomous.

---

[113] Pilate illustrated the deficiency with his immortal question: "What is truth?" Which he asked immediately before handing Christ over to be crucified.

[114] "...because it was to come to pass that the religion of the Christian priesthood should especially thrive in France, God provided that among the Gauls too their tribal priests, called Druids, should lay down the law of all Gaul." *De Regno*, 113.

They differ both in their configuration and their ends: the Church is oriented toward the spiritual needs of the faithful, and the State toward the temporal common good.[115] They are each self-governing and autonomous, as the Church has repeatedly confirmed.[116] Even the powerful statement of Pope Gelasius I, if we quote it further, elaborates that "the ministers of religion, recognizing the supremacy granted you from heaven in matters affecting the public order, obey your laws, lest otherwise they might obstruct the course of secular affairs by irrelevant considerations."[117]

The Church does not even insist on one particular governmental form over another, stating that "the Church respects the legitimate autonomy of the democratic order and is not entitled to express preferences for this or that institutional or constitutional solution." Nor does she propose specific, technical solutions to economic and political problems.[118]

Yet, while it has always been the habit of the Church to acknowledge and allow space for the temporal power, the State has not often been so gracious. The reason for the lack of reciprocity is not hard to comprehend, even if it has unfortunate results. It goes back to the historical inability, or unwillingness, of those called to action to understand or accept the vocation of those called to knowledge.

e. The Expansionist Character of the Temporal Power

The Gospel says:

> "Now it came to pass as they went, that he entered into a certain town: and a certain woman named Martha, received

---

[115] *Compendium of the Social Doctrine of the Church*, 424.
[116] *Gaudium et Spes*, 76.
[117] Letter of Gelasius I.
[118] *Caritas in Veritate*, 9; CA, 43; OA, 4.

him into her house. And she had a sister called Mary, who sitting also at the Lord's feet, heard his word. But Martha was busy about much serving. Who stood and said: Lord, hast thou no care that my sister hath left me alone to serve? speak to her therefore, that she help me. And the Lord answering, said to her: Martha, Martha, thou art careful, and art troubled about many things: But one thing is necessary. Mary hath chosen the best part, which shall not be taken away from her."[119]

Of this, the anonymous medieval class, *The Cloud of Unknowing*, comments:

"As Martha complained of Mary her sister, so unto this day all actives complain of contemplatives. For if there be a man or a woman in any company of this world that feeleth stirred through grace and by counsel to forsake all outward business...their own brethren and their sisters, and all their next friends, with many other that know not their stirrings nor that manner of living that they set them to, with a great complaining spirit shall rise upon them, and say sharply unto them that they are idle. And as fast they will reckon up many false tales..."[120]

This is the essence of the Gospel conflict between Mary and Martha: that there are two vocations—active and contemplative, action or knowledge. Christ affirmed that Mary, who represents the life of contemplation and knowledge, had chosen the better part, not because Martha's labors were in vain, but because the vocation of contemplation is of a higher order. The second lesson is this: that those called to the higher order cannot justify themselves to those persons called to a life of action, because, while the higher

---

[119] Luke 10:38-42.
[120] *The Cloud of Unknowing*, ch. 18.

comprehends the lower order, the lower cannot fully comprehend the higher. This is why Christ had to intervene by means of his authority rather than by means of explanation.

This conflict plays itself out through all history in the perennial tendency of the temporal power to deny the validity and supremacy of spiritual knowledge. Governments tend to expand and, unable to comprehend the value of the clergy and its vocation, will deny and then usurp the role of the spiritual authority. This process has had its recurrences in India, between the Kshatriyas and the Brahmins; it happened in medieval Christendom through the Reformation, where princes overthrew the clergy; it happened in Japan as well.

Several consequences naturally follow from this process. First, the spiritual authority cannot perform its duties when divorced from its proper position in the hierarchy. This means that when its place is usurped, it is not simply demoted but is rendered impotent and its duties made impossible. Second, once the Church is rendered unable to perform that which falls within its sphere, the State, as the only remaining social authority, absorbs these functions into itself.

f. The Shrinking Sphere of Faith and Morals

We are then left with a situation in which the temporal power—the State—is all-encompassing. Because this is our present arrangement, and because we can hardly conceive of any other, we have learned to associate virtually all social functions with the State alone.

We are shocked, then, to hear that the Church has something important to say about political activity, social organization, economic activity, and war. We cannot understand that these matters, while they do concern the State, also have their moral aspects which must be guided by the principles of the Church if they are to remain functional and healthy. Thus, while aloof as far as concrete commercial operations are concerned, the Church has very distinct economic principles which are meant to *inform* and *guide* commercial activity. And so we must instantly suspect allegations that the Church, whose concern is faith and morals, ought not speak on economics, when in reality "every economic decision has a moral consequence."[121]

We now sit in a situation in which the Church is told at every step that it is interfering in "worldly affairs" that do not fall within its sphere of concern. And yet, it would seem that we are hard pressed to find a single area that actually qualifies as pertaining to "faith and morals." Nothing, it seems, pertains to faith and morals any longer.

g. The Church's Aim is Man as Body and Soul

Now we must approach the same subject from a different perspective, looking not at what the Church's role *was*, or *has become*, but instead asking what the Church see its role to be. What does the Church expect to achieve through her assertions? Why not just be satisfied to remain in the sanctuaries, administering sacraments and preaching sermons, aloof from all the tumult and strife? In short: What is the Church's *aim*, in her own words and from her point of view? In this way we approach the heart of Catholic Social Doctrine.

The answer can be found in the simple maxim given to us by St. Thomas: "Grace presupposes nature."

This may initially seem like one of those "finer points of pointless philosophy," of which Erasmus complained, but if we pause on the fact we will see that it has profound consequences. If it is true that "grace presupposes nature," it means that the life of grace somehow is intertwined with the created world. Such an idea provides an important perspective, especially since we tend to see "nature" as the enemy and grace as a force operating in opposition to it. But that is

---

[121] *Caritas in Veriate*, 37.

the negative side of the coin, to which there is also a positive side, which Aquinas refuses to leave un-emphasized:

The created world was intended as a medium for the realization of love, for "man was created to love and everything else was created to make love possible."[122] As such, it does assist man in his spiritual realization. To relate this again to the words of Aquinas, nature acts as a substrate for the action of grace.

One obvious conclusion we can draw from this is that man's socio-economic situation, while it does not absolutely determine his personal development, can certainly help or hurt it. Materially speaking, there is a necessary minimum required by him in order to give proper attention to the development of his uniquely human faculties. If he is strained beyond certain tolerable limits, *it matters for his spiritual growth.* This being the case, how could the Church not be concerned?

Man is both body *and* soul. His visible and invisible parts affect one another, and it was the recognition of this essential truth that gave birth of Catholic Social Teaching in 1891 when Leo XIII wrote *Rerum Novarum.* He was not reacting to some abstract theological error, but to a concrete socio-economic issue. That is why the subtitle to the letter was "On the Conditions of the Working Class."

Man's spiritual development was being threatened by social conditions that had gone outside that "tolerable limit" and had begun to threaten man's development on every level. While the Church leaves things untouched that are functioning properly, the increasingly violent nature of industrialism brought the issue well within the purview of the Church. A response then becomes a matter of duty. Pope Pius XI said as much in *Quadragesimo Anno*:

---

[122] *The Cloud of Unknowing,* 4.

"...it must be said with all truth that nowadays the conditions of the social and economic life are such that vast multitudes of men can only with great difficulty pay attention to that one thing necessary, namely, their eternal salvation."

The documents of Vatican II agree whole-heartedly on this point, speaking of the "new stage of history" and its "crisis of growth":

"Profound and rapid changes are spreading by degrees around the whole world. Triggered by the intelligence and creative energies of man, these changes recoil upon him, upon his decisions and desires, both individual and collective, and upon his manner of thinking and acting with respect to things and to people. Hence we can already speak of a true cultural and social transformation, one which has repercussions on man's religious life as well."[123]

h. The Pastoral Mission of the Church

It falls to the Church, then, to "scrutinize the signs of the times...interpreting them in light of the Gospel...in language intelligible to each generation."[124] This relates to the continuity and renewal of CST which we mentioned earlier.

Christ said to Peter: *Feed by sheep.* This is the sole duty of the Church, as she repeats the words of Paul: "Woe to me if I do not preach the Gospel!"[125] "Man is the primary and fundamental way for the Church."[126] Her mission is therefore *pastoral*, coming to man's aid when the forces of the world overwhelm him, or when he overwhelms himself. She knows that he "painstakingly searches for a

---

[123] *Gaudium et Spes*, 4.
[124] Ibid.
[125] 1 Corinthians 9:16.
[126] *Redemptor Hominis*, 14.

better world, without working with equal zeal for the betterment of his own spirit."[127] And so she comes to his side as his only competent physician, as the true "expert in humanity."

> It is not possible for the Church to remain indifferent to social matters.[128] Canon Law itself announces that "To the Church belongs the right always and everywhere to announce moral principles, including those pertaining to the social order, and to make judgments on any human affairs to the extent that they are required by the fundamental rights of the human person or the salvations of souls."[129]

Although it so often confounds her accusers, the Church cannot renounce her ministry to man. And like the Seven Sacraments, she has something to contribute in each phase and order of his life:

> "The Catholic Church, that imperishable handiwork of our All-Merciful God, has for her immediate and natural purpose the saving of souls and securing our happiness in heaven. Yet in regard to things temporal she is the source of benefits as manifold and great as if the chief end of her existence were to ensure the prospering of our earthly life."[130]

> "[T]here resides in Us the right and duty to pronounce with supreme authority upon social and economic matters …Even though economics and moral science employs each its own principles in its own sphere, it is, nevertheless, an error to say that the economic and moral orders are so distinct from and alien to each other that the former depends in no way on the latter."[131]

---

[127] *Gaudium et Spes*, 4.
[128] *Evangelii Nuntiandi*, 34.
[129] *Cod of Canon Law*, canon 747, 2.
[130] *Immortale Dei*, 1.
[131] *Quadragesimo Anno*, 41-42.

i. The Vision of the Structure

From the pursuit of this mission, the body Catholic Social Doctrine was born, aptly summarized in the *Compendium* as "an updated doctrinal 'corpus'...[that] builds up gradually, as the Church, in the fullness of the word revealed by Christ Jesus and with the assistance of the Holy Spirit (cf. Jn 14:16, 26; 16:13-15), reads events as they unfold in the course of history."[132]

Catholicism, therefore, does not deal in "conservative" religion. It does not simply retain what truths it has, but penetrates ever more deeply into the Truth. Its doctrine, and in particular its social doctrine, is *additive* rather than *conservative,* and this is proof of its life. It is not a petrified relic in a shrine to be observed: it lives and grows and guides.

And where does it guide?

> "The Church's social doctrine indicates the path to follow for a society reconciled and in harmony through justice and love, a society that anticipates in history, in a preparatory and prefigurative manner, the 'new heavens and a new earth in which righteousness dwells' (2 Peter 3:13)."[133]

This is the path to the City of God, which Augustine admitted could not be disentangled from the City of Man, but which was our goal and end nonetheless:

> "The mortal course of the two cities, the heavenly and the earthly, [are] intermingled from beginning to end. One of them, the earthly, has created for herself from any source she pleased, even out of men, false gods to worship with sacrifice; the other, a heavenly pilgrim on earth, does not

---

[132] *Sollicitudo Rei Socialis,* 1.
[133] *Compendium of the Social Doctrine of the Church,* 82.

create false gods, but is herself created by the true God, whose sacrifice she is herself."[134]

The Church may be imagined as an architect, laboring through history to discern the outline of the Holy City. Her Social Doctrine is that portion of the divine blueprint she has discovered so far.

6. The Office of the Pope

a. The Necessity of the Priesthood

The Church adheres in the Priesthood, and it is absurd to imagine, as the Protestants do, that the Church depends on the book and not on the men who wrote it, assembled it, and guard it to this day, for as Nicholas Gomez-Davila has said: "Christ did not leave books, but Apostles."

For this reason St. Cyprian of Carthage could write in A.D. 254:

> "You ought to know that the bishop is in the Church, and the Church in the bishop; and if anyone be not with the bishop, then he is not in the Church, nor those who flatter themselves in vain and creep in, not having peace with God's priests, and think that they communicate secretly with some; while the Church, which is catholic and one, is not cut nor divided, but is indeed connected and bound together by the cement of priests who cohere with one another."[135]

It is for this reason that apostolic succession is so important to the Church, and has been since St. Irenaeus of Lyons wrote to defend it in A.D. 189:

> "It is within the power of all, in every church, who may wish to see the truth, to contemplate clearly the Tradition of

---

[134] Augustine, *City of God*, 18.
[135] *Letters*, 68:8.

the apostles manifested throughout the whole world; and we are in a position to reckon up those who were instituted bishops in the churches by the apostles, and to demonstrate the succession of these men to our own times...

"For it is a matter of necessity that every church agree with this Church, on account of its preeminent authority, that is, the faithful everywhere, because the apostolic Tradition has been preserved continuously..."

"It is incumbent to obey the presbyters who are in the Church—those who, as I have shown, possess the succession from the apostles..."

"True knowledge is the doctrine of the apostles, and the ancient constitution of the Church throughout all the world, and the distinctive manifestation of the body of Christ according to the successions of bishops..."[136]

And perhaps this *living* aspect of the body of Christ, and the Catholic attitude toward it, was best stated by St. Jerome in A.D. 367:

"Far be it from me to censure the successors of the apostles, who with holy words consecrate the body of Christ, and who make us Christians."[137]

b. Peter the Rock

And just as, among the apostles themselves, one was chosen,[138] so also, after the fashion of the twelve, one bishop is chosen to lead the Church in every period.

---

[136] *Against Heresies*, 3:3:1-4, 3:4:1, 4:26:2, 4:33:8.
[137] *Letters*, 14:8.
[138] *Matthew*, 16:18.

"The Lord says to Peter: 'I say to you,' he says, 'that you are Peter, and upon this rock I will build my Church, and the gates of hell will not overcome it. And to you I will give the keys of the kingdom of heaven; and whatever things you bind on earth shall be bound also in heaven, and whatever you loose on earth, they shall be loosed also in heaven' [Matt. 16:18–19]). ... On him [Peter] he builds the Church, and to him he gives the command to feed the sheep [John 21:17], and although he assigns a like power to all the apostles, yet he founded a single chair [*cathedra*], and he established by his own authority a source and an intrinsic reason for that unity. Indeed, the others were also what Peter was [i.e., apostles], but a primacy is given to Peter, whereby it is made clear that there is but one Church and one chair. So too, all [the apostles] are shepherds, and the flock is shown to be one, fed by all the apostles in single-minded accord. If someone does not hold fast to this unity of Peter, can he imagine that he still holds the faith? If he [should] desert the chair of Peter upon whom the Church was built, can he still be confident that he is in the Church?"[139]

To turn again to St. Jerome:

> "As I follow no leader save Christ, so I communicate with none but your blessedness, that is, with the chair of Peter. For this, I know, is the rock on which the Church is built!"[140]

c. The Authority of the Pope

The authority of the pope, which causes the American to cringe, has been a bastion and a comfort to the Christian giants of the past.

---

[139] St. Cyprian of Carthage, *Unity of the Catholic Church* 4; first edition (Treatise 1:4), A.D. 251.
[140] *Letters,* 15:2, A.D. 376.

Jerome once lamented factions, and found comfort by "clinging to the Chair of Peter," that is to say, staying faithful to the Pope.

Likewise, St. Augustine cited a reliance on the papacy as one of the profundities that kept him in the Church:

> "There are many other things that most justly keep me in her bosom...The succession of priests keeps me, beginning from the very seat of the apostle Peter, to whom the Lord, after his Resurrection, put in charge of feeding his sheep, down to the present episcopate."[141]

And the same saint, in the midst of a controversy, said in exasperation:

> "On this matter two councils have already been sent to the Apostolic See [the bishop of Rome], and from there replies too have come. The matter is at an end; would that the error too might be at an end!"[142]

Rather than continue to weary the reader with the witness of centuries, let us simply refer to the form of communication which he is more familiar with—the Encyclical document—and observe that much of the docility and deference these saints showed toward the popes of days gone by are rightly owed to these statements as well. In the words of Pope Pius XII (1950):

> "Nor must it be thought that what is expounded in Encyclical Letters does not of itself demand consent, since in writing such Letters the Popes do not exercise the supreme power of their Teaching Authority. For these matters are taught with the ordinary teaching authority, of which it is true to say: 'He who heareth you, heareth me'; and generally what is expounded and inculcated in Encyclical Letters

---

[141] *Against the Letter of mani Called 'The Foundation,'* 4:5, A.D. 397.
[142] *Letters*, 17, A.D. 414.

105

already for other reasons appertains to Catholic doctrine. But if the Supreme Pontiffs in their official documents purposely pass judgment on a matter up to that time under dispute, it is obvious that that matter, according to the mind and will of the Pontiffs, cannot be any longer considered a question open to discussion among theologians."[143]

No one would attempt to say that every decision the pope should make is indeed "infallible," but it seems to us that there is little danger today of any American person making a mistake in that regard. On the contrary, the American tendency is to move in the opposite direction and to imagine every utterance proceeding from Rome as "just one man's opinion." That is the present danger, and it is a great error indeed. For this reason we dwell on it, and not on its opposite.

d. The Office and the Man

In order to ease the acceptance of this "hard truth"—obedience due the Roman Pontiff—it is helpful to recall an ancient principle that, along with the rise of personality and popular government, has been largely lost to history. We are referring to the distinction between an office and the man who holds the office.

To summarize the doctrine, it basically states that a ruler may be evil, but that does not mean that his rule is evil. In fact, Gerald de Barri (1146-1220) explains that: "Princely power is necessary for men, since where there is no government the people will come to ruin,"[144] and St. Thomas Aquinas also tells us that rulers are necessary. Since human rulers are necessary, and since sin is present in every man, we can see immediately that imperfection in a ruler is not of itself justification for refusing obedience to his authority.

---

[143] *Humani Generis,* 20.
[144] *De Instrucione Principum,* 1.

This is because the authority of the man comes from his office, and it is his office that his subjects respect when they obey him, and not the ruler himself. Thus, goodness *is not* the test of authority, as Wyclif would later suggest. A ruler who acquires his office justly may be an evil man and yet compel his subject to obedience. In the words of St. Bonaventure: "that evil men who rule well should be in authority is no evil to the State."

And so it seems that, as distasteful an act as it was, President Bill Clinton's adultery had no bearing on his legitimacy as a ruler.

e. Infallibility

Infallibility is one of the most misunderstood doctrines of the Church, and so we owe it a few comments and clarifications.

First, we must remind Catholics that infallibility is not the same thing as "impeccability," which is to say the pope can and does sin and make incorrect statements from time to time. Moreover, infallibility being an attribute of the Church that merely manifests itself in the figure of the pope, it is also shared to some degree by the bishops. According to Vatican II:

> "Although the individual bishops do not enjoy the prerogative of infallibility, they can nevertheless proclaim Christ's doctrine infallibly. This is so, even when they are dispersed around the world, provided that while maintaining the bond of unity among themselves and with Peter's successor, and while teaching authentically on a matter of faith or morals, they concur in a single viewpoint as the one which must be held conclusively. This authority is even more clearly verified when, gathered together in an ecumenical council, they are teachers and judges of faith and morals for the universal Church. Their definitions must then be adhered to with the submission of faith."[145]

107

However, the prerogative of infallibility belongs in a special way to the pope as head of the bishops (Matt. 16:17–19; John 21:15–17). It is a charism the pope,

> "enjoys in virtue of his office, when, as the supreme shepherd and teacher of all the faithful, who confirms his brethren in their faith (Luke 22:32), he proclaims by a definitive act some doctrine of faith or morals. Therefore his definitions, of themselves, and not from the consent of the Church, are justly held irreformable, for they are pronounced with the assistance of the Holy Spirit, an assistance promised to him in blessed Peter."[146]

f. Aspects of the Divinity: Knowledge, Power, Compassion

We already reviewed the re-orientation that took place through the Second Vatican Council, and this, as far as we are concerned, justifies that *apparent*—but not *actual*—compromise made by the Church with respect to Modernism. What we wish to mention here, however, is that this same "change in posture" should naturally express itself through the person of the Pontiff. We should expect to see popes who conduct themselves in a different manner and employ a different pastoral approach than those who came before them, and this should not be interpreted as opposition or contradiction, but as the sign of the Living Church which follows its lost sheep even into the storm.

To understand what we mean, let us take an example far removed from the Christian context but which nonetheless displays useful correspondences to our situation.

It is well-known that in the Buddhist tradition the *Dalai Lama*, usually residing in Tibet, is considered a "Living Buddha," that is to

---

[145] *Lumen Gentium,* 25.
[146] Ibid.

say he is an "incarnation" of the Buddha. What is less-known is that, within the same tradition, there has simultaneously existed a *Panchen Lama* and another office, the *Bogda Kahn* of Mongolia, each of whom can be considered a "Living Buddha" in his own right. This amounts to three incarnations living simultaneously. Is this a contradiction?

This is not a contradiction but is in fact the Buddhist counterpart to the Christian Trinity, and conveys in its way the same truth: *that divinity is not susceptible to one definite representation.*

Each of the three *Lamas* represents a different aspect of Divinity. The *Dalai Lama*, with whom nearly all Westerners are familiar, represents the "realization" of the Buddha's compassion or mercy. The *Tashi Lama*, capable of great feats of science, and representing the Buddha's wisdom, hence his significant role in selecting the new *Dalai Lama*. Finally, there is the great *Bogda Khan*, a warrior figure, representing power and material strength.

Why, then, do we mention this point? Because, taking the obvious differences into account, this Buddhist tradition offers a helpful illustration that is, in its own way, mirrored in Christianity through the popes, which in their personalities may exemplify one or another of these aspects (or none at all, as we have seen). And why should we not expect this sort of variation in he who holds such an office? Each age and each civilization requires shepherds capable of communicating the message they most need, and which is most appropriate to the time. The changes we see from one pope to another may be interpreted less as a weakness than as a powerful proof of the authenticity of the office.

Let us return to Buddhism for one more observation:

As the modern world has unfolded, the two Lamas representing power and knowledge have either receded into a subordinate role, as with the *Panchen Lama*, or else, as in the case of the *Bogda Kahn*, disappeared altogether. The only remaining Lama, at least the only one the modern West can comprehend, is the *Dalai Lama*—the Lama of compassion. And not only can the modern world comprehend them, but they are drawn to him.

In a similar way, the Papacy too has been occupied by men of formidable worldly power, such as Julius II ("The Warrior Pope"). Later in history, it was occupied by men of great wisdom and intellect, from Leo XIII to St. John Paul II. Is it really so surprising— is it really incongruous with the nature of the Creator—that today, in this particular period, as if Providence itself had called him forth, that a Pontiff who manifests God's compassion, mercy, and love would appear on the scene? We hope this gives the reader pause.

It is for this reason that we papists should find in Pope Francis's papacy not some sort of "revolution" or "reversal" in the direction of the Church's development, but rather a fulfillment of a necessity. This progression from Power to Intellect to Compassion (Julius to Leo to Francis) may be interpreted as nothing more than the historical manifestation of the Trinity.

After all, it should be clear by now that ours is not an "age of knowledge," much less do we need "Warrior Popes" in the nuclear age. No, for our period nothing seems more necessary than the realization of Christ's mercy—his compassionate love for a broken humanity.

This, in our eyes, is the "anagogical" meaning of the present papacy. Pope Francis is a man moving amid the ruins of Christendom, tending to the wounded, and wounded souls do not need—at least not most immediately—knowledge or grand displays of power. They need tenderness and mercy. Francis himself said precisely the same thing:

"I see clearly that the thing the church needs most today is the ability to heal wounds and to warm the hearts of the faithful ... I see the church as a field hospital after battle."[147]

It is because Pope Francis seems to us to have appeared on the scene at just the right time, in order to provide just the style of guidance and direction that our epoch requires, that we can earnestly recommend to the American Catholic a sort of "Neo-Papism"—a new-found sense of devotion and obedience to our Pastoral leader.

This is not an attempt to divinize his humanity; we do not wish to ignore his sinful nature, a nature which he shares with every other human being on earth; nor are we arguing for the blind, fanatical obedience that comes with a "cult of personality." Quite the contrary, we recommend this new (or, more accurately, this very old) posture of docility toward the Pope simply because his Office is the Office of St. Peter—the Rock. He is our Chief Pastor, and it would do the individualistic, rationalistic, American soul a great deal of spiritual good to finally begin treating him as such.

This is a chaotic age. Let us follow the example of St. Jerome, who, even with his astounding intellect and position within the Church, felt that there was no better way of anchoring oneself to the Truth than by clinging to the Roman Throne.

---

[147] Interview with *America Magazine*, September 30, 2013.

III. Positions

There you have it—our thesis has been presented. We argue for a religious anti-revolution—a return to obedience, and to a childlike willingness to be taught by our Mater et Magistra.

In order to illustrate more particularly and with concrete examples the merit of the approach we have suggested, this section provides a wide range of statements from various popes, many of them from Pope Francis himself, that today are contentious in American political conversation. The intent here is to show the positions that our "Neo-Papist" would be inclined to take on each subject.

Against Capitalism

"Property, that is, 'capital,' has undoubtedly long been able to appropriate too much to itself. Whatever was produced, whatever returns accrued, capital claimed for itself, hardly leaving to the worker enough to restore and renew his strength. For the doctrine was preached that all accumulation of capital falls by an absolutely insuperable economic law to the rich, and that by the same law the workers are given over and bound to perpetual want, to the scantiest of livelihoods. It is true, indeed, that things have not always and everywhere corresponded with this sort of teaching of the so-called Manchesterian Liberals; yet it cannot be denied that economic social institutions have moved steadily in that direction." – Pope Pius XI[148]

"We have seen that it is unacceptable to say that the defeat of so-called 'Real Socialism' leaves capitalism as the only model of economic organization." – Pope St. John Paul II[149]

"The tension between East and West is an opposition... between two concepts of the development of individuals and peoples, both

---

[148] *Quadragesimo Anno*, 54.
[149] *Centesimus Annus*, 35.

concepts being imperfect and in need of radical correction... This is one of the reasons why the Church's social doctrine adopts a critical attitude towards both liberal capitalism and Marxist collectivism." – Pope St. John Paul II[150]

"…in every social situation of this type, there is a confusion or even a reversal of the order laid down from the beginning by the words of the Book of Genesis: *man is treated as an instrument of production*, whereas he--he alone, independently of the work he does--ought to be treated as the effective subject of work and its true maker and creator. Precisely this reversal of order, whatever the programme or name under which it occurs, should rightly be called "capitalism"-in the sense more fully explained below. Everybody knows that capitalism has a definite historical meaning as a system, an economic and social system, opposed to "socialism" or "communism". But in the light of the analysis of the fundamental reality of the whole economic process-first and foremost of the production structure that work is-it should be recognized that the error of early capitalism can be repeated wherever man is in a way treated on the same level as the whole complex of the material means of production, as an instrument and not in accordance with the true dignity of his work-that is to say, where he is not treated as subject and maker, and for this very reason as the true purpose of the whole process of production." – Pope St. John Paul II[151]

"…it is right to confirm all the effort with which the Church's teaching has striven and continues to strive always to ensure the priority of work and, thereby, man's character as a *subject* in social life and, especially, in the dynamic *structure of the whole economic process.* From this point of view the position of "rigid" capitalism continues to remain unacceptable, namely the position that defends

---

[150] *Sollicitudo Rei Socialis.*
[151] *Laborem Exercens*, 7.

the exclusive right to private ownership of the means of production as an untouchable "dogma" of economic life." – Pope St. John Paul II[152]

Against the Fictitious Separation of Economics and Morality

"Strict and watchful moral restraint enforced vigorously by governmental authority could have banished these enormous evils and even forestalled them; this restraint, however, has too often been sadly lacking. For since the seeds of a new form of economy were bursting forth just when the principles of rationalism had been implanted and rooted in many minds, there quickly developed a body of economic teaching far removed from the true moral law, and, as a result, completely free rein was given to human passions." – Pope Pius XI[153]

"Then, the conviction that the economy must be autonomous, that it must be shielded from "influences" of a moral character, has led man to abuse the economic process in a thoroughly destructive way. In the long term, these convictions have led to economic, social and political systems that trample upon personal and social freedom, and are therefore unable to deliver the justice that they promise." – Pope Benedict XVI[154]

"All of this can be summed up by repeating once more that economic freedom is only one element of human freedom. When it becomes autonomous, when man is seen more as a producer or consumer of goods than as a subject who produces and consumes in order to live, then economic freedom loses its necessary relationship to the human person and ends up by alienating and oppressing him." – Pope St. John Paul II[155]

---

[152] *Laborem Exercens,* 14.
[153] *Quadragesimo Anno,* 133.
[154] *Caritas in Veritate,* 34.
[155] *Centesimus Annus,* 39.

Against Cultural, Economic, and Religious Proselytism[156]

"It is not by proselytizing that the Church grows, but 'by attraction'." – Pope Francis[157]

"Convert you? Proselytism is solemn nonsense. You have to meet people and listen to them." – Pope Francis[158]

"To be called by Jesus, to be called to evangelize, and third: to be called to promote the culture of encounter – In many places, generally speaking, due to the economic humanism that has been imposed in the world, the culture of exclusion, of rejection, is spreading. There is no place for the elderly or for the unwanted child; there is no time for that poor person in the street. At times, it seems that for some people, human relations are regulated by two modern "dogmas": efficiency and pragmatism...Have the courage to go against the tide of this culture of efficiency, this culture of waste. Encountering and welcoming everyone, solidarity – a word that is being hidden by this culture, as if it were a bad word – solidarity and fraternity: these are what make our society truly human. Be servants of communion and of the culture of encounter!...Watch over me, Mother, when I am disoriented, and lead me by the hand. May you spur us on to meet our many brothers and sisters who are on the outskirts, who are hungry for God but have no one to proclaim him.

---

[156] Americans tend to operate with an aggressively evangelistic mentality, not only with respect to religion but also regarding their institutions, economic attitudes, and their general worldview. Remember Maritain's observation above—that Americans *need to be loved*, and Tocqueville's observation that if Americans are not praised, they will praise themselves. This results in a society that pictures themselves as the great "City on a Hill," and that therefore assumes that all other cultures could be improved by becoming more like themselves. In its secular form, this "proselytism mania" manifests itself as attempts to make the rest of the world democratic and capitalist, like us. In its religious form it results in Evangelicalism with its youth group "mission" vacations. But such is not the Catholic way.

[157] *Evangelii Gaudium,* 15.

[158] From a letter to Eugenio Scalfari, founder of *La Repubblica*.

May you not force us out of our homes, but encourage us to go out so that we may be disciples of the Lord." – Pope Francis[159]

"In order to proclaim Jesus, Paul made himself 'a slave to all.' Evangelizing means bearing personal witness to the love of God, it is overcoming our selfishness, it is serving by bending down to wash the feet of our brethren, as Jesus did." – Pope Francis[160]

Against Minimalistic Pro-Life-ism[161]

"I encourage you, then, my brothers, to confront the challenging issues of our time. Ever present within each of them is life as gift and responsibility. The future freedom and dignity of our societies depends on how we face these challenges. The innocent victim of abortion, children who die of hunger or from bombings, immigrants who drown in the search for a better tomorrow, the elderly or the

---

[159] *Address at Prayer Vigil with the Young People*, July 27, 2013.

[160] *Homily on the Occasion of XXVIII World Youth Day*, July 28, 2013.

[161] The Church has always taught the dignity and value of human life at every state. The Pro-Life Movement is to be applauded in that they have held tightly to this position. However, we have also observed a significant inconsistency in their rhetoric and actions that suggests, at best, a certain superficiality, and at worst downright hypocrisy. That is to say they rightly abhor abortion, on the grounds that it displays a disregard for human life, and then they turn around and defend social policies that disregard human dignity and in fact foster the very conditions that make abortion attractive. This is due primarily to the fact that "Pro-Lifers" often identify with the Republican Party which, due to its own inner contradictions, remains blind to human degradation *in all* of its forms. And so this party stakes out a "moral high ground" on the abortion issue while remaining indifferent to a host of other evils that are connected it. Here again Pope Francis is our teacher, for he is ready and willing to condemn abortion, but he never condemns abortion by itself, as if it were an act carried out in a vacuum. Always Pope Francis speaks of abortion *and its surrounding evils*, namely the "culture of waste," the "throwaway culture," poverty, and the general disregard for human life in other countries and in situations far removed from our own. He speaks of the need for a resounding and unreserved "Yes!" to life in all its stages and forms. This "Whole Life" mentality is much more effective and appropriate than a "Pro-Life" political platform that is, in the end, merely "pro-fetus."

sick who are considered a burden, the victims of terrorism, wars, violence and drug trafficking, the environment devastated by man's predatory relationship with nature – at stake in all of this is the gift of God, of which we are noble stewards but not masters. It is wrong, then, to look the other way or to remain silent." – Pope Francis[162]

"A widespread mentality of the useful, the 'culture of waste' that today enslaves the hearts and minds of so many, comes at a very high cost: it asks for the elimination of human beings, especially if they are physically or socially weaker. Our response to this mentality is a decisive and unreserved 'yes' to life. 'The first right of the human person is his life. He has other goods and some are more precious, but this one is fundamental — the condition of all the others.' Things have a price and can be sold, but people have a dignity; they are worth more than things and are above price. So often we find ourselves in situations where we see that what is valued the least is life. That is why concern for human life in its totality has become in recent years a real priority for the Church's Magisterium, especially for the most defenseless; i.e., the disabled, the sick, the newborn, children, the elderly, those whose lives are most defenseless." – Pope Francis[163]

"The scourge of abortion is an attack on life. Leaving our brothers on the boats in the Sicilian channel is an attack on life. Death in the workplace is an attack on life because the minimal security conditions are not respected. Death by malnutrition is an attack on life. Terrorism, war, violence and also euthanasia are an attack on life. Loving life means always to take care of the other, to wish him well, to cultivate and respect his transcendent dignity." – Pope Francis[164]

---

[162] *Meeting with the Bishops of the United States of America*, September 23, 2015.
[163] *Address to Meeting of the International Federation of Catholic Medical Associations* (9/20/13).
[164] *Address to Participants in Meeting of the Science and Life Association*

"...it is frightful even to think there are children, victims of abortion, who will never see the light of day; children being used as soldiers, abused and killed in armed conflicts; and children being bought and sold in that terrible form of modern slavery which is human trafficking, which is a crime against humanity." – Pope Francis[165]

Against the Megalopolis

"In big cities, beneath the roar of traffic, beneath 'the rapid pace of change,' so many faces pass by unnoticed because they have no 'right' to be there, no right to be part of the city. They are the foreigners, the children who go without schooling, those deprived of medical insurance, the homeless, the forgotten elderly. These people stand at the edges of our great avenues, in our streets, in deafening anonymity. They become part of an urban landscape which is more and more taken for granted, in our eyes, and especially in our hearts." – Pope Francis[166]

"Nowadays, for example, we are conscious of the disproportionate and unruly growth of many cities, which have become unhealthy to live in, not only because of pollution caused by toxic emissions but also as a result of urban chaos, poor transportation, and visual pollution and noise. Many cities are huge, inefficient structures, excessively wasteful of energy and water. Neighbourhoods, even those recently built, are congested, chaotic and lacking in sufficient green space. We were not meant to be inundated by cement, asphalt, glass and metal, and deprived of physical contact with nature." – Pope Francis[167]

(5/30/15).

[165] *Address to Members of the Diplomatic Corps* (1/13/14).
[166] *Homily at Mass at Madison Square Garden* (9/25/15).
[167] *Laudato Si'*, 44.

"In the unstable neighbourhoods of mega-cities, the daily experience of overcrowding and social anonymity can create a sense of uprootedness which spawns antisocial behaviour and violence." – Pope Francis[168]

Against Biocentrism and Anthropocentrism

"This situation has led to a constant schizophrenia, wherein a technocracy which sees no intrinsic value in lesser beings coexists with the other extreme, which sees no special value in human beings. But one cannot prescind from humanity. There can be no renewal of our relationship with nature without a renewal of humanity itself. There can be no ecology without an adequate anthropology. When the human person is considered as simply one being among others, the product of chance or physical determinism, then 'our overall sense of responsibility wanes.' A misguided anthropocentrism need not necessarily yield to 'biocentrism,' for that would entail adding yet another imbalance, failing to solve present problems and adding new ones. Human beings cannot be expected to feel responsibility for the world unless, at the same time, their unique capacities of knowledge, will, freedom and responsibility are recognized and valued.

"Nor must the critique of a misguided anthropocentrism underestimate the importance of interpersonal relations. If the present ecological crisis is one small sign of the ethical, cultural and spiritual crisis of modernity, we cannot presume to heal our relationship with nature and the environment without healing all fundamental human relationships. Christian thought sees human beings as possessing a particular dignity above other creatures; it thus inculcates esteem for each person and respect for others. Our openness to others, each of whom is a "thou" capable of knowing, loving and entering into dialogue, remains the source of our nobility

---

[168] *Laudato Si', 149.*

as human persons. A correct relationship with the created world demands that we not weaken this social dimension of openness to others, much less the transcendent dimension of our openness to the "Thou" of God. Our relationship with the environment can never be isolated from our relationship with others and with God. Otherwise, it would be nothing more than romantic individualism dressed up in ecological garb, locking us into a stifling immanence." – Pope Francis[169]

Against Cultural Uniformity

"Here our model is not the sphere, which is no greater than its parts, where every point is equidistant from the centre, and there are no differences between them. Instead, it is the polyhedron, which reflects the convergence of all its parts, each of which preserves its distinctiveness. Pastoral and political activity alike seek to gather in this polyhedron the best of each. There is a place for the poor and their culture, their aspirations and their potential. Even people who can be considered dubious on account of their errors have something to offer which must not be overlooked. It is the convergence of peoples who, within the universal order, maintain their own individuality; it is the sum total of persons within a society which pursues the common good, which truly has a place for everyone." – Pope Francis[170]

"When properly understood, cultural diversity is not a threat to Church unity. The Holy Spirit, sent by the Father and the Son, transforms our hearts and enables us to enter into the perfect communion of the blessed Trinity, where all things find their unity. He builds up the communion and harmony of the people of God. The same Spirit is that harmony, just as he is the bond of love between the Father and the Son. It is he who brings forth a rich

---

[169] *Laudato Si'*, 118-119.
[170] *Evangelii Gaudium*, 236.

variety of gifts, while at the same time creating a unity which is never uniformity but a multifaceted and inviting harmony." – Pope Francis[171]

"Cooperation for development must not be concerned exclusively with the economic dimension: it offers a wonderful opportunity for encounter between cultures and peoples. If the parties to cooperation on the side of economically developed countries — as occasionally happens — fail to take account of their own or others' cultural identity, or the human values that shape it, they cannot enter into meaningful dialogue with the citizens of poor countries. If the latter, in their turn, are uncritically and indiscriminately open to every cultural proposal, they will not be in a position to assume responsibility for their own authentic development." – Pope Benedict XVI[172]

"Today the possibilities of *interaction between cultures* have increased significantly, giving rise to new openings for intercultural dialogue: a dialogue that, if it is to be effective, has to set out from a deep-seated knowledge of the specific identity of the various dialogue partners. Let it not be forgotten that the increased commercialization of cultural exchange today leads to a twofold danger. First, one may observe a *cultural eclecticism* that is often assumed uncritically: cultures are simply placed alongside one another and viewed as substantially equivalent and interchangeable." – Pope Benedict XVI[173]

Against Arbitrary Freedom

"When all restraints are removed by which men are kept on the narrow path of truth, their nature, which is already inclined to evil, propels them to ruin. Then truly 'the bottomless pit' is open from

---

[171] *Evangelii Gaudium,* 117.
[172] *Caritas in Veritate,* 59.
[173] *Caritas in Veritate,* 26.

which John saw smoke ascending which obscured the sun, and out of which locusts flew forth to devastate the earth. Thence comes transformation of minds, corruption of youths, contempt of sacred things and holy laws -- in other words, a pestilence more deadly to the state than any other. Experience shows, even from earliest times, that cities renowned for wealth, dominion, and glory perished as a result of this single evil, namely immoderate freedom of opinion, license of free speech, and desire for novelty." – Pope Gregory XVI[174]

"Some are so carried away that they contentiously assert that the flock of errors arising from them is sufficiently compensated by the publication of some book which defends religion and truth. Every law condemns deliberately doing evil simply because there is some hope that good may result. Is there any sane man who would say poison ought to be distributed, sold publicly, stored, and even drunk because some antidote is available and those who use it may be snatched from death again and again?" – Pope Gregory XVI[175]

"We must now consider briefly liberty of speech, and liberty of the press. It is hardly necessary to say that there can be no such right as this, if it be not used in moderation, and if it pass beyond the bounds and end of all true liberty. For right is a moral power which - as We have before said and must again and again repeat - it is absurd to suppose that nature has accorded indifferently to truth and falsehood, to justice and injustice. Men have a right freely and prudently to propagate throughout the State what things soever are true and honorable, so that as many as possible may possess them; but lying opinions, than which no mental plague is greater, and vices which corrupt the heart and moral life should be diligently repressed by public authority, lest they insidiously work the ruin of the State. The excesses of an unbridled intellect, which unfailingly end in the oppression of the untutored multitude, are no less rightly

---

[174] *Mirari Vos*, 14.
[175] *Mirari Vos*, 15.

controlled by the authority of the law than are the injuries inflicted by violence upon the weak. And this all the more surely, because by far the greater part of the community is either absolutely unable, or able only with great difficulty, to escape from illusions and deceitful subtleties, especially such as flatter the passions. If unbridled license of speech and of writing be granted to all, nothing will remain sacred and inviolate; even the highest and truest mandates of natures, justly held to be the common and noblest heritage of the human race, will not be spared. Thus, truth being gradually obscured by darkness, pernicious and manifold error, as too often happens, will easily prevail. Thus, too, license will gain what liberty loses; for liberty will ever be more free and secure in proportion as license is kept in fuller restraint. In regard, however, to all matter of opinion which God leaves to man's free discussion, full liberty of thought and of speech is naturally within the right of everyone; for such liberty never leads men to suppress the truth, but often to discover it and make it known." – Pope Leo XIII[176]

"It is in the light of the dignity of the human person — a dignity which must be affirmed for its own sake — that reason grasps the specific moral value of certain goods towards which the person is naturally inclined. And since the human person cannot be reduced to a freedom which is self-designing, but entails a particular spiritual and bodily structure, the primordial moral requirement of loving and respecting the person as an end and never as a mere means also implies, by its very nature, respect for certain fundamental goods, without which one would fall into relativism and arbitrariness." – Pope St. John Paul II[177]

---

[176] *Libertas*, 23.
[177] *Veritatis Splendor*, 48.

Against the Profit-Motive

"Profit is a regulator of the life of a business, but it is not the only one; *other human and moral factors* must also be considered which, in the long term, are at least equally important for the life of a business." – Pope St. John Paul II[178]

"Profit is useful if it serves as a means towards an end that provides a sense both of how to produce it and how to make good use of it. Once profit becomes the exclusive goal, if it is produced by improper means and without the common good as its ultimate end, it risks destroying wealth and creating poverty." – Pope Benedict XVI[179]

"There are millions of men and women and even children who are slaves to labor! At this time there are slaves, they are exploited, slaves to labor and this is against God and against the dignity of the human person! The obsession with economic profit and technical hyper-efficiency put the human rhythms of life at risk." – Pope Francis[180]

Against Consumerism, Waste, and the Throwaway Culture

"A given culture reveals its overall understanding of life through the choices it makes in production and consumption. It is here that *the phenomenon of consumerism* arises. In singling out new needs and new means to meet them, one must be guided by a comprehensive picture of man which respects all the dimensions of his being and which subordinates his material and instinctive dimensions to his interior and spiritual ones. If, on the contrary, a direct appeal is made to his instincts — while ignoring in various ways the reality of

---

[178] *Centesimus Annus*, 35.
[179] *Caritas in Veritate*, 21.
[180] *General Audience*, August 12, 2015.

the person as intelligent and free — then *consumer attitudes* and *life-styles* can be created which are objectively improper and often damaging to his physical and spiritual health. Of itself, an economic system does not possess criteria for correctly distinguishing new and higher forms of satisfying human needs from artificial new needs which hinder the formation of a mature personality." – Pope St. John Paul II[181]

"Men and women are sacrificed to the idols of profit and consumption: it is the 'culture of waste.' If a computer breaks it is a tragedy, but poverty, the needs and dramas of so many people end up being considered normal." – Pope Francis[182]

"Today's economic mechanisms promote inordinate consumption, yet it is evident that unbridled consumerism combined with inequality proves doubly damaging to the social fabric." – Pope Francis[183]

"The greed of consumerism, which leads to waste, is an ugly virus which, among other things, makes us end up even more tired than before. It harms true labor and consumes life. Irregular rhythms of celebration often make victims of the young." – Pope Francis[184]

"We have become somewhat accustomed to this throwaway culture: too often the elderly are discarded! But now we have all these young people with no work, they too are suffering the effects of the throwaway culture. We must rid ourselves of this habit of throwing away. No! The culture of inclusion, the culture of encounter, making an effort to bring everyone into society!" – Pope Francis[185]

---

[181] *Centesimus Annus*, 36.
[182] *General Audience*, June 5, 2013.
[183] *Evangelii Gaudium*, 60.
[184] *General Audience*, August 12, 2015.
[185] *Meeting with Journalists during the Flight to Brazil*, July 22, 2013.

"We cannot be indifferent to those suffering from hunger, especially children, when we think of how much food is wasted every day in many parts of the world immersed in what I have often termed 'the throwaway culture.' Unfortunately, what is thrown away is not only food and dispensable objects, but often human beings themselves, who are discarded as 'unnecessary.' " – Pope Francis[186]

"New ideologies, characterized by rampant individualism, egocentrism and materialistic consumerism, weaken social bonds, fuelling that "throw away" mentality which leads to contempt for, and the abandonment of, the weakest and those considered 'useless.' " – Pope Francis[187]

Against Intergenerational Disconnect

"We are now faced with a philosophy and a practice which exclude the two ends of life that are most full of promise for peoples. They exclude the elderly, obviously. You could easily think there is a kind of hidden euthanasia, that is, we don't take care of the elderly; but there is also a cultural euthanasia, because we don't allow them to speak, we don't allow them to act. And there is the exclusion of the young. The percentage of our young people without work, without employment, is very high and we have a generation with no experience of the dignity gained through work. This civilization, in other words, has led us to exclude the two peaks that make up our future. As for the young, they must emerge, they must assert themselves, the young must go out to fight for values, to fight for these values; and the elderly must open their mouths, the elderly must open their mouths and teach us!" – Pope Francis[188]

"Human life, the person is no longer perceived as a primary value to be respected and protected, especially if poor or disabled, if not yet

[186] *Address to Members of the Diplomatic Corps*, January 13, 2014.
[187] *General Audience*, December 8, 2013.
[188] *Address at Meeting with Young People from Argentina*, July 25, 2013.

useful - such as the unborn child - or no longer needed - such as the elderly." – Pope Francis[189]

"It is true that the global crisis harms the young. I read last week the percentage of the young without work. Just think that we risk having a generation that has never worked, and yet it is through work that a person acquires dignity by earning bread. The young, at this moment, are in crisis. We have become somewhat accustomed to this throwaway culture: too often the elderly are discarded! But now we have all these young people with no work, they too are suffering the effects of the throwaway culture. We must rid ourselves of this habit of throwing away. No! The culture of inclusion, the culture of encounter, making an effort to bring everyone into society!" – Pope Francis[190]

"God did not want an idol to be at the center of the world but man, men and women who would keep the world going with their work. Yet now, in this system devoid of ethics, at the center there is an idol and the world has become an idolater of this "god-money". ... Money is in command! Money lays down the law! It orders all these things that are useful to it, this idol. And what happens? To defend this idol all crowd to the center and those on the margins are done down, the elderly fall away, because there is no room for them in this world!" – Pope Francis[191]

"Do you open your hearts to the memories that your grandparents pass on? Grandparents are like the wisdom of the family, they are the wisdom of a people." – Pope Francis[192]

"Such an economy is not only desirable and necessary, but also possible. It is no utopia or chimera. It is an extremely realistic

[189] *General Audience on UN World Environment Day*, June 5, 2013.
[190] *Meeting with Journalists during the Flight to Brazil*, July 22, 2013.
[191] *Meeting with Workers in Cagliari, Sardinia*, September 22, 2013.
[192] *Speech in St. Peter's Square*, October 26, 2013.

prospect. We can achieve it. The available resources in our world, the fruit of the intergenerational labors of peoples and the gifts of creation, more than suffice for the integral development of 'each man and the whole man.' " – Pope Francis[193]

Against Usury

"Hence, by degrees it has come to pass that working men have been surrendered, isolated and helpless, to the hardheartedness of employers and the greed of unchecked competition. The mischief has been increased by rapacious usury, which, although more than once condemned by the Church, is nevertheless, under a different guise, but with like injustice, still practiced by covetous and grasping men." – Pope Leo XIII[194]

"[Vulnerable sectors of the population] should be protected from the risk of usury and from despair. The weakest members of society should be helped to defend themselves against usury, just as poor peoples should be helped to derive real benefit from micro-credit, in order to discourage the exploitation that is possible in these two areas." – Pope Benedict XVI[195]

"I hope that these institutions may intensify their commitment alongside the victims of usury, a dramatic social ill...When a family has nothing to eat, because it has to make payments to usurers, this is not Christian, it is not human! This dramatic scourge in our society harms the inviolable dignity of the human person." – Pope Francis[196]

---

[193] *Address at the Second World Meeting of Popular Movements,* July 9, 2015.
[194] *Rerum Novarum,* 3.
[195] *Caritas in Veritate,* 65.
[196] *Address to National Council of Anti-Usury Foundations.*

Against Confusing License with Liberty

"You are a servant of the Lord and you are a freedman of the Lord. Do not go looking for a liberation which will lead you far from the house of your liberator!" – St. Augustine[197]

"In the same way the Church cannot approve of that liberty which begets a contempt of the most sacred laws of God, and casts off the obedience due to lawful authority, for this is not liberty so much as license, and is most correctly styled by St. Augustine the "liberty of self ruin," and by the Apostle St. Peter the "cloak of malice." Indeed, since it is opposed to reason, it is a true slavery, "for whosoever committeth sin is the slave of sin." On the other hand, that liberty is truly genuine, and to be sought after, which in regard to the individual does not allow men to be the slaves of error and of passion, the worst of all masters…" – Pope Leo XIII[198]

"But many there are who follow in the footsteps of Lucifer, and adopt as their own his rebellious cry, "I will not serve"; and consequently substitute for true liberty what is sheer and most foolish license. Such, for instance, are the men belonging to that widely spread and powerful organization, who, usurping the name of liberty, style themselves liberals." – Pope Leo XIII[199]

Against Labor as Commodity

"Labor…is not a mere commodity. On the contrary, the worker's human dignity in it must be recognized. It therefore cannot be bought and sold like a commodity." – Pope Pius XI[200]

---

[197] *Enarratio in Psalmum XCIX*, 7.
[198] *Immortale Dei*, 37.
[199] *Libertas*, 14.
[200] *Quadragesimo Anno*, 83.

"There are goods which by their very nature cannot and must not be bought or sold. Certainly the mechanisms of the market offer secure advantages: they help to utilize resources better; they promote the exchange of products; above all they give central place to the person's desires and preferences, which, in a contract, meet the desires and preferences of another person. Nevertheless, these mechanisms carry the risk of an "idolatry" of the market, an idolatry which ignores the existence of goods which by their nature are not and cannot be mere commodities." – Pope St. John Paul II[201]

Against Population Control

"To blame population growth instead of extreme and selective consumerism on the part of some, is one way of refusing to face the issues. It is an attempt to legitimize the present model of distribution, where a minority believes that it has the right to consume in a way which can never be universalized, since the planet could not even contain the waste products of such consumption." – Pope Francis[202]

Against Secularism

"For, men living together in society are under the power of God no less than individuals are, and society, no less than individuals, owes gratitude to God who gave it being and maintains it and whose ever-bounteous goodness enriches it with countless blessings. Since, then, no one is allowed to be remiss in the service due to God, and since the chief duty of all men is to cling to religion in both its reaching and practice-not such religion as they may have a preference for, but the religion which God enjoins, and which certain and most clear marks show to be the only one true religion -it is a public crime to act as though there were no God. So, too, is it a sin for the State not

---

[201] *Centesimus Annus*, 40.
[202] *Laudato Si'*, 50.

to have care for religion as a something beyond its scope, or as of no practical benefit; or out of many forms of religion to adopt that one which chimes in with the fancy; for we are bound absolutely to worship God in that way which He has shown to be His will. All who rule, therefore, would hold in honour the holy name of God, and one of their chief duties must be to favour religion, to protect it, to shield it under the credit and sanction of the laws, and neither to organize nor enact any measure that may compromise its safety." – Pope Leo XIII[203]

"The process of secularization tends to reduce the faith and the Church to the sphere of the private and personal. Furthermore, by completely rejecting the transcendent, it has produced a growing deterioration of ethics, a weakening of the sense of personal and collective sin, and a steady increase in relativism. These have led to a general sense of disorientation, especially in the periods of adolescence and young adulthood which are so vulnerable to change." – Pope Francis[204]

Against Ideology[205]

"In ideologies there is not Jesus: in his tenderness, his love, his meekness. And ideologies are rigid, always. Of every sign: rigid. And when a Christian becomes a disciple of the ideology, he has lost the faith: he is no longer a disciple of Jesus, he is a disciple of this attitude of thought." – Pope Francis[206]

---

[203] *Immortale Dei*, 6.
[204] *Evangelii Gaudium*, 64.
[205] Pope Francis speaks of ideology as a "distilled faith," passed through a filter with only the superficialities retained.
[206]

http://en.radiovaticana.va/storico/2013/10/17/pope_francis_prayer_keeps_u s_from_losing_faith/en1-738101

"While the income of a minority is increasing exponentially, that of the majority is crumbling. This imbalance results from ideologies which uphold the absolute autonomy of markets and financial speculation, and thus deny the right of control to States, which are themselves charged with providing for the common good." – Pope Francis[207]

"Before all else, the Gospel invites us to respond to the God of love who saves us, to see God in others and to go forth from ourselves to seek the good of others. Under no circumstance can this invitation be obscured! All of the virtues are at the service of this response of love. If this invitation does not radiate forcefully and attractively, the edifice of the Church's moral teaching risks becoming a house of cards, and this is our greatest risk. It would mean that it is not the Gospel which is being preached, but certain doctrinal or moral points based on specific ideological options. The message will run the risk of losing its freshness and will cease to have 'the fragrance of the Gospel.' " – Pope Francis[208]

"...we are witnessing a renewal of the liberal ideology. This current asserts itself both in the name of economic efficiency, and for the defense of the individual against the increasingly overwhelming hold of organizations, and as a reaction against the totalitarian tendencies of political powers. Certainly, personal initiative must be maintained and developed. But do not Christians who take this path tend to idealize liberalism in their turn, making it a proclamation in favor of freedom?" – Pope Paul VI[209]

"The smallest, the weakest, the poorest soften us: they have the "right" to take our heart and soul. Yes, they are our brothers and sisters and as such we must love and care for them. When this

---

[207] *Audience with Ambassadors (regarding financial reform)*, May 16, 2013.
[208] *Evangelii Gaudium*, 39.
[209] *Octogesima Adveniens*, 35.

happens, when the poor are like family members, our own Christian fraternity comes to life again. Christians, in fact, go to meet the poor and the weak not to obey an ideological programme, but because the word and the example of the Lord tell us that we are all brothers and sisters." – Pope Francis[210]

For a Proper Understanding of Charity and Justice

"Charity goes beyond justice, because to love is to give, to offer what is "mine" to the other; but it never lacks justice, which prompts us to give the other what is "his", what is due to him by reason of his being or his acting. I cannot "give" what is mine to the other, without first giving him what pertains to him in justice. If we love others with charity, then first of all we are just towards them. Not only is justice not extraneous to charity, not only is it not an alternative or parallel path to charity: justice is inseparable from charity, and intrinsic to it. Justice is the primary way of charity or, in Paul VI's words, "the minimum measure" of it…" – Pope Benedict XVI[211]

For Private Property in the Service of the Common Good

"Therefore, those whom fortune favors are warned that riches do not bring freedom from sorrow and are of no avail for eternal happiness, but rather are obstacles; that the rich should tremble at the threatenings of Jesus Christ - threatenings so unwonted in the mouth of our Lord - and that a most strict account must be given to the Supreme Judge for all we possess. The chief and most excellent rule for the right use of money is one the heathen philosophers hinted at, but which the Church has traced out clearly, and has not only made known to men's minds, but has impressed upon their lives. It rests on the principle that it is one thing to have a right to

---

[210] *General Audience*, February 18, 2015.
[211] *Caritas in Veritate*, 6.

the possession of money and another to have a right to use money as one wills. Private ownership, as we have seen, is the natural right of man, and to exercise that right, especially as members of society, is not only lawful, but absolutely necessary...But if the question be asked: How must one's possessions be used? - the Church replies without hesitation in the words of the same holy Doctor: 'Man should not consider his material possessions as his own, but as common to all, so as to share them without hesitation when others are in need...True, no one is commanded to distribute to others that which is required for his own needs and those of his household; nor even to give away what is reasonably required to keep up becomingly his condition in life, 'for no one ought to live other than becomingly.' But, when what necessity demands has been supplied, and one's standing fairly taken thought for, it becomes a duty to give to the indigent out of what remains over." – Pope Leo XIII[212]

"Christian tradition has never upheld this right [private property] as absolute and untouchable. On the contrary, it has always understood this right within the broader context of the right common to all to use the goods of the whole of creation: *the right to private property is subordinated to the right to common use,* to the fact that goods are meant for everyone." – Pope St. John Paul II[213]

For Distributive Justice

"[T]he hiring of labor and the conduct of trade are concentrated in the hands of comparatively few; so that a small number of very rich men have been able to lay upon the teeming masses of the laboring poor a yoke little better than that of slavery itself." – Pope Leo XIII[214]

"...the social doctrine of the Church has unceasingly highlighted the importance of *distributive justice* and *social justice* for the market

---

[212] *Rerum Novarum,* 22.
[213] *Laborem Exercens,* 14.
[214] *Rerum Novarum,* 3.

economy, not only because it belongs within a broader social and political context, but also because of the wider network of relations within which it operates...it must be borne in mind that grave imbalances are produced when economic action, conceived merely as an engine for wealth creation, is detached from political action, conceived as a means for pursuing justice through redistribution...*Economic life* undoubtedly requires *contracts*, in order to regulate relations of exchange between goods of equivalent value. But it also needs *just laws* and *forms of redistribution* governed by politics." – Pope Benedict XVI[215]

"Working for a just distribution of the fruits of the earth and human labor is not mere philanthropy. It is a moral obligation. For Christians, the responsibility is even greater: it is a commandment. It is about giving to the poor and to peoples what is theirs by right. – Pope Francis[216]

For the Preferential Option for the Poor

"Still, when there is question of defending the rights of individuals, the poor and badly off have a claim to especial consideration. The richer class have many ways of shielding themselves, and stand less in need of help from the State; whereas the mass of the poor have no resources of their own to fall back upon, and must chiefly depend upon the assistance of the State. And it is for this reason that wage-earners, since they mostly belong in the mass of the needy, should be specially cared for and protected by the government." – Pope Leo XIII[217]

"The Pope loves everyone, rich and poor alike, but he is obliged in the name of Christ to remind all that the rich must help, respect and promote the poor." – Pope Francis[218]

---

[215] *Caritas in Veritate*, 35-37.
[216] *Address at the Second World meeting of Popular Movements.*
[217] *Rerum Novarum*, 37.

136

"The poor person, when loved, "is esteemed as of great value",[168] and this is what makes the authentic option for the poor differ from any other ideology, from any attempt to exploit the poor for one's own personal or political interest. Only on the basis of this real and sincere closeness can we properly accompany the poor on their path of liberation." – Pope Francis[219]

For Mercy toward Immigrants and Refugees

"Another aspect of integral human development that is worthy of attention is the phenomenon of *migration*. This is a striking phenomenon because of the sheer numbers of people involved, the social, economic, political, cultural and religious problems it raises, and the dramatic challenges it poses to nations and the international community. We can say that we are facing a social phenomenon of epoch-making proportions that requires bold, forward-looking policies of international cooperation if it is to be handled effectively... The phenomenon, as everyone knows, is difficult to manage; but there is no doubt that foreign workers, despite any difficulties concerning integration, make a significant contribution to the economic development of the host country through their labour...They must not, therefore, be treated like any other factor of production. Every migrant is a human person who, as such, possesses fundamental, inalienable rights that must be respected by everyone and in every circumstance." – Pope Benedict XVI[220]

"Immigrants dying at sea, in boats which were vehicles of hope and became vehicles of death. That is how the headlines put it. When I first heard of this tragedy a few weeks ago, and realized that it happens all too frequently, it has constantly come back to me like a painful thorn in my heart. So I felt that I had to come here today, to

[218] *Evangelii Gaudium,* 58.
[219] *Evangelii Gaudium,* 199.
[220] *Caritas in Veritate,* 62.

pray and to offer a sign of my closeness, but also to challenge our consciences lest this tragedy be repeated. Please, let it not be repeated!

"Where is your brother?" His blood cries out to me, says the Lord. This is not a question directed to others; it is a question directed to me, to you, to each of us. These brothers and sisters of ours were trying to escape difficult situations to find some serenity and peace; they were looking for a better place for themselves and their families, but instead they found death. How often do such people fail to find understanding, fail to find acceptance, fail to find solidarity. And their cry rises up to God! Once again I thank you, the people of Lampedusa, for your solidarity. I recently listened to one of these brothers of ours. Before arriving here, he and the others were at the mercy of traffickers, people who exploit the poverty of others, people who live off the misery of others. How much these people have suffered! Some of them never made it here." – Pope Francis[221]

"While it is true that migrations often reveal failures and shortcomings on the part of States and the international community, they also point to the aspiration of humanity to enjoy a unity marked by respect for differences, by attitudes of acceptance and hospitality which enable an equitable sharing of the world's goods, and by the protection and the advancement of the dignity and centrality of each human being." – Pope Francis[222]

"It is necessary to respond to the globalization of migration with the globalization of charity and cooperation, in such a way as to make the conditions of migrants more humane. At the same time, greater efforts are needed to guarantee the easing of conditions, often

---

[221] *Homily during Visit to Lampedusa*, July 8, 2013.
[222] *Message for World Day of Migrants and Refugees 2014*, August 5, 2013.

brought about by war or famine, which compel whole peoples to leave their native countries." – Pope Francis[223]

For Respect for Creation

"Equally worrying is *the ecological question* which accompanies the problem of consumerism and which is closely connected to it. In his desire to have and to enjoy rather than to be and to grow, man consumes the resources of the earth and his own life in an excessive and disordered way. At the root of the senseless destruction of the natural environment lies an anthropological error, which unfortunately is widespread in our day. Man, who discovers his capacity to transform and in a certain sense create the world through his own work, forgets that this is always based on God's prior and original gift of the things that are. Man thinks that he can make arbitrary use of the earth, subjecting it without restraint to his will, as though it did not have its own requisites and a prior God-given purpose, which man can indeed develop but must not betray. Instead of carrying out his role as a co-operator with God in the work of creation, man sets himself up in place of God and thus ends up provoking a rebellion on the part of nature, which is more tyrannized than governed by him." – Pope St. John Paul II[224]

"The way humanity treats the environment influences the way it treats itself, and vice versa. This invites contemporary society to a serious review of its life-style, which, in many parts of the world, is prone to hedonism and consumerism, regardless of their harmful consequences. What is needed is an effective shift in mentality which can lead to the adoption of *new life-styles* 'in which the quest for truth, beauty, goodness and communion with others for the sake of common growth are the factors which determine consumer

---

[223] *Message for the 101st World Day of Migrants and Refugees*, September 3, 2014.
[224] *Centesimus Annus*, 37.

choices, savings and investments.' Every violation of solidarity and civic friendship harms the environment, just as environmental deterioration in turn upsets relations in society. Nature, especially in our time, is so integrated into the dynamics of society and culture that by now it hardly constitutes an independent variable." – Pope Benedict XVI[225]

For Cooperation Over Competition

"These concepts present profit as the chief spur to economic progress, free competition as the guiding norm of economics, and private ownership of the means of production as an absolute right, having no limits nor concomitant social obligations.

"This unbridled liberalism paves the way for a particular type of tyranny, rightly condemned by Our predecessor Pius XI, for it results in the 'international imperialism of money.'

"Such improper manipulations of economic forces can never be condemned enough; let it be said once again that economics is supposed to be in the service of man." – Pope Paul VI[226]

"…both workers and employers should regulate their mutual relations in accordance with the principle of human solidarity and Christian brotherhood. Unrestricted competition in the liberal sense, and the Marxist creed of class warfare; are clearly contrary to Christian teaching and the nature of man." – Pope St. John XXIII[227]

"In proclaiming the principles for a solution of the worker question, Pope Leo XIII wrote: 'This most serious question demands the attention and the efforts of others.' He was convinced that the grave problems caused by industrial society could be solved only by cooperation between all forces. This affirmation has become a

---

[225] *Caritas in Veritate*, 51.
[226] *Populorum Progressio*, 26.
[227] *Mater et Magistra,* 23.

permanent element of the Church's social teaching, and also explains why Pope John XXIII addressed his Encyclical on peace to 'all people of good will.' Pope Leo, however, acknowledged with sorrow that the ideologies of his time, especially Liberalism and Marxism, rejected such cooperation." – Pope St. John Paul II[228]

"Hence, by degrees it has come to pass that working men have been surrendered, isolated and helpless, to the hardheartedness of employers and the greed of unchecked competition." – Pope Leo XIII[229]

"Today everything comes under the laws of competition and the survival of the fittest, where the powerful feed upon the powerless. As a consequence, masses of people find themselves excluded and marginalized: without work, without possibilities, without any means of escape." – Pope Francis[230]

"With respect to States themselves, Our predecessors have constantly taught, and We wish to lend the weight of Our own authority to their teaching, that nations are the subjects of reciprocal rights and duties. Their relationships, therefore, must likewise be harmonized in accordance with the dictates of truth, justice, willing cooperation, and freedom. The same law of nature that governs the life and conduct of individuals must also regulate the relations of political communities with one another." – Pope St. John XXIII[231]

For Divine Sovereignty[232]

"There is one lawgiver and judge, who is able to destroy and deliver." – The Apostle James[233]

---

[228] *Centesimus Annus*, 60.
[229] *Rerum Novarum*, 3.
[230] *Evangelii Gaudium*, 53.
[231] *Pacem in Terris*, 80.
[232] For a society that acknowledges transcendence, or God, it is inconceivable that any group of men should "make" the law, and if such a theory does arise,

"And, since where religion has been removed from civil society, and the doctrine and authority of divine revelation repudiated, the genuine notion itself of justice and human right is darkened and lost, and the place of true justice and legitimate right is supplied by material force, thence it appears why it is that some, utterly neglecting and disregarding the surest principles of sound reason, dare to proclaim that "the people's will, manifested by what is called public opinion or in some other way, constitutes a supreme law, free from all divine and human control; and that in the political order accomplished facts, from the very circumstance that they are accomplished, have the force of right." But who, does not see and clearly perceive that human society, when set loose from the bonds of religion and true justice, can have, in truth, no other end than the purpose of obtaining and amassing wealth, and that (society under such circumstances) follows no other law in its actions, except the unchastened desire of ministering to its own pleasure and interests?"
– Pope Pius IX[234]

---

which indeed it has in the form of popular sovereignty, then an unprecedented form of absolutism appears on the horizon. This is because a monarch of old who was, or at least had to pretend as if he was, subject to God, had to tether his laws to God's law, for his role was to apply God's law, and not to make his own. Under popular sovereignty, however, where the will of enough people is the only standard of legislation, the tether is broken and the law is limited only by the imagination of the human person, which is a terrifying prospect. Not only does this result in a proliferation of thousands of laws that the average citizen cannot even begin to comprehend, but it also means that the approach to law will fluctuate according to the fad and fashion of each generation, as we see today in the United States, which has decided of late that a person can, indeed, change their own gender. This is why the popes argue that the only sane theory of law is one that derives from above. While, for the reasons we have already mentioned, it is unrealistic to expect modern secular states to completely re-evaluate their theories of sovereignty and law, we should nonetheless be aware of the truth of Divine Sovereignty. This provides us with a legitimate standard by which to judge our present arrangement.

[233] *James,* 4:12.
[234] *Quanta Cura,* 4.

"Indeed, very many men of more recent times, walking in the footsteps of those who in a former age assumed to themselves the name of philosophers, say that all power comes from the people; so that those who exercise it in the State do so not as their own, but as delegated to them by the people, and that, by this rule, it can be revoked by the will of the very people by whom it was delegated. But from these, Catholics dissent, who affirm that the right to rule is from God, as from a natural and necessary principle." – Pope Leo XIII[235]

"Those who believe civil society to have risen from the free consent of men, looking for the origin of its authority from the same source, say that each individual has given up something of his right,(15) and that voluntarily every person has put himself into the power of the one man in whose person the whole of those rights has been centered. But it is a great error not to see, what is manifest, that men, as they are not a nomad race, have been created, without their own free will, for a natural community of life. It is plain, moreover, that the pact which they allege is openly a falsehood and a fiction, and that it has no authority to confer on political power such great force, dignity, and firmness as the safety of the State and the common good of the citizens require. Then only will the government have all those ornaments and guarantees, when it is understood to emanate from God as its august and most sacred source." – Pope Leo XIII[236]

"For an unwillingness to attribute the right of ruling to God, as its Author, is not less than a willingness to blot out the greatest splendor of political power and to destroy its force. And they who say that this power depends on the will of the people err in opinion first of all; then they place authority on too weak and unstable a foundation. For the popular passions, incited and goaded on by these

---

[235] *Diuturnum*, 5.
[236] *Diuturnum*, 12.

opinions, will break out more insolently; and, with great harm to the common weal, descend headlong by an easy and smooth road to revolts and to open sedition. In truth, sudden uprisings and the boldest rebellions immediately followed in Germany the so-called Reformation, the authors and leaders of which, by their new doctrines, attacked at the very foundation religious and civil authority; and this with so fearful an outburst of civil war and with such slaughter that there was scarcely any place free from tumult and bloodshed. From this heresy there arose in the last century a false philosophy - a new right as it is called, and a popular authority, together with an unbridled license which many regard as the only true liberty. Hence we have reached the limit of horrors, to wit, communism, socialism, nihilism, hideous deformities of the civil society of men and almost its ruin." – Pope Leo XIII[237]

"[I]n the constitution of the State such as We have described, divine and human things are equitably shared; the rights of citizens assured to them, and fenced round by divine, by natural, and by human law; the duties incumbent on each one being wisely marked out, and their fulfilment fittingly insured...In political affairs, and all matters civil, the laws aim at securing the common good, and are not framed according to the delusive caprices and opinions of the mass of the people, but by truth and by justice." – Pope Leo XIII[238]

For Reform and Regulation of Financial Institutions

"Both the regulation of the financial sector, so as to safeguard weaker parties and discourage scandalous speculation, and experimentation with new forms of finance, designed to support development projects, are positive experiences that should be further explored and encouraged, highlighting *the responsibility of the investor.*" – Pope Benedict XVI[239]

---

[237] *Diuturnum*, 23.
[238] *Immortale Dei*, 17-18.

"I encourage financial experts and political leaders to ponder the words of one of the sages of antiquity: 'Not to share one's wealth with the poor is to steal from them and to take away their livelihood. It is not our own goods which we hold, but theirs.' A financial reform open to such ethical considerations would require a vigorous change of approach on the part of political leaders. I urge them to face this challenge with determination and an eye to the future, while not ignoring, of course, the specifics of each case. Money must serve, not rule!" – Pope Francis[240]

For the Universal Application of Rights

"In a world in which a lot is said about rights, how often is human dignity actually trampled upon! In a world in which so much is said about rights, it seems that the only thing that has any rights is money. Dear brothers and sisters, we are living in a world where money commands. We are living in a world, in a culture where the fixation on money holds sway." – Pope Francis[241]

For Solidarity and Subsidiarity

The Church teaches both solidarity and subsidiarity, and teaches them a harmony. Thus, we ought to make a point never to speak of them in isolation, which, by omitting one half of the balance, usually results in disorder:

"We have said that the State must not absorb the individual or the family; both should be allowed free and untrammelled action so far as is consistent with the common good and the interest of others. Rulers should, nevertheless, anxiously safeguard the community and all its members; the community, because the conservation thereof is

---

[239] *Caritas in Veritate,* 65.
[240] *Evangelii Gaudium,* 57-58.
[241] *Address to Participants in the Plenary of the Pontifical Council for the Pastoral Care of Migrants and Itinerant People,* May 25, 2013.

so emphatically the business of the supreme power, that the safety of the commonwealth is not only the first law, but it is a government's whole reason of existence." – Pope Leo XIII[242]

"The principle of subsidiarity must remain closely linked to the principle of solidarity and vice versa, since the former without the latter gives way to social privatism, while the latter without the former gives way to paternalist social assistance that is demeaning to those in need." – Pope Benedict XVI[243]

For the Social Kingship of Christ

"It would be a grave error, on the other hand, to say that Christ has no authority whatever in civil affairs, since, by virtue of the absolute empire over all creatures committed to him by the Father, all things are in his power. Nevertheless, during his life on earth he refrained from the exercise of such authority, and although he himself disdained to possess or to care for earthly goods, he did not, nor does he today, interfere with those who possess them. *Non eripit mortalia qui regna dat caelestia.* Thus the empire of our Redeemer embraces all men…

"When once men recognize, both in private and in public life, that Christ is King, society will at last receive the great blessings of real liberty, well-ordered discipline, peace and harmony. Our Lord's regal office invests the human authority of princes and rulers with a religious significance; it ennobles the citizen's duty of obedience. It is for this reason that St. Paul, while bidding wives revere Christ in their husbands, and slaves respect Christ in their masters, warns them to give obedience to them not as men, but as the vicegerents of Christ; for it is not meet that men redeemed by Christ should serve their fellow-men. "You are bought with a price; be not made the

---

[242] *Rerum Novarum,* 35.
[243] *Caritas in Veritate,* 58.

bond-slaves of men."[32] If princes and magistrates duly elected are filled with the persuasion that they rule, not by their own right, but by the mandate and in the place of the Divine King, they will exercise their authority piously and wisely, and they will make laws and administer them, having in view the common good and also the human dignity of their subjects. The result will be a stable peace and tranquillity, for there will be no longer any cause of discontent. Men will see in their king or in their rulers men like themselves, perhaps unworthy or open to criticism, but they will not on that account refuse obedience if they see reflected in them the authority of Christ God and Man. Peace and harmony, too, will result; for with the spread and the universal extent of the kingdom of Christ men will become more and more conscious of the link that binds them together, and thus many conflicts will be either prevented entirely or at least their bitterness will be diminished." – Pope Pius XI[244]

Epilogue: On Courage

It behooves us to end with some words on courage—the virtue that we believe is required in order to adopt the posture of docility, devotion, and obedience to the Teaching Church and its Pontiff. This is because obedience requires more courage than rebellion. Rebellion is easy, and in fact the average American citizen has thoroughly trained to be proud of his prodigality. But prodigality is not a virtue. It was Lucifer who was the coward; it was the Archangel Michael who was courageous.

Aleksander Solzhenitsyn claimed the following:

> "A decline in courage may be the most striking feature which an outside observer notices in the West in our days. The Western world has lost its civil courage, both as a whole and separately, in each country, each government, each

---

[244] *Quas Primas*, 17-19.

political party and of course in the United Nations. Such a decline in courage is particularly noticeable among the ruling groups and the intellectual elite, causing an impression of loss of courage by the entire society. Of course there are many courageous individuals but they have no determining influence on public life…Should one point out that from ancient times decline in courage has been considered the beginning of the end?"[245]

There is an old parable regarding some servants who, being trusted by their master with varying quantities of money, each acted in a different fashion. Two of the three invested it, and surrendered the profit to their master. The third man, however, buried his portion, and returned precisely the amount that he was given. When he does this, his master condemns him as a coward, and has him thrown out into the darkness. From this parable we can assume two things, one about the master, and the other about the servant. About the master, we can say that he obviously prefers courageous error to cowardly omission, and that this fact ought to have been clear to everyone who knew him. About the servant, we can assume that his fear drove him to an act of the second kind, which explains why it was inexcusable. This, then, is a parable about courage, and it seems to us that it is a perfect representation of the modern world.

Fear is paralyzing. As Frank Herbert, the master of science fiction, once put it: "fear is the mind-killer." And this is the precise truth, because a person acting in fear loses his capacity for judgment precisely insofar as he is affected by his fear. In fear, he does things that, in a peaceful frame of mind, he'd have found ridiculous. This is why we would expect that, if fear were to become a generalized condition in a civilization, knowledge itself would begin to deteriorate.

---

[245] Aleksander Solzhenitsyn, Harvard Commencement Address delivered on June 8, 1978.

Knowledge has a character of command. If something is true, and if we know it is true, we must act in accordance with it. Men across all various creeds agree at least on that, and this is why the immoralist does not claim the right to ignore morality, but rather denies its existence. No one acknowledges a truth and at the same time denies the obligation—the duty—it imposes. And so again, in ages of fear, truth, because of its imperious character, is the most despised of things.

It is like a small child who chooses not to ask his mother a question because he knows he isn't going to like the answer. The modern man is just such a figure—the questions every man in history was ready to ask, are by him denied as valid. He wants nothing to do with them.

Cowardice says: "Only this—and only if I must."

One has to completely ignore the past in order to worship the future.

When Spengler famously wrote that "optimism is cowardice," it was just this sort of thing he was describing. He was not so much condemning a "positive attitude" as he was condemning a very specific kind of positive attitude, the one adopted in order to avoid the severe realities of life, because it is only through these realities that courage and honor can be teased out of existence:

> "We are born into this time and must bravely follow the path to the destined end. There is no other way. Our duty is to hold on to the lost position, without hope, without rescue, like that Roman soldier whose bones were found in front of a door in Pompeii, who, during the eruption of Vesuvius, died at his post because they forgot to relieve him. That is greatness. That is what it means to be a thoroughbred. The honorable end is the one thing that cannot be taken from a man."[246]

149

We could proceed through a number of "types," familiar to all, to illustrate this omnipresent and enslaving fear: Think of the man who stockpiles weaponry in his basement, and rages in the streets about his "rights," and who imagines the day when he will have to do battle with his government when they come to steal these "rights" from him. Clearly this behavior is an expression of paranoia, an extreme and enslaving condition of *fear*.

This boils down to a fear of people, and a fear of the vulnerability required by human communion. It is a rejection of communion. The pure individualist is not brave—he is hiding. He wants to be alone, because aloneness allows us to escape vulnerability. Rene Guenon was right when he observed that the root of human fear is not a fear of being alone, but rather the inescapable knowledge that we are not, and cannot ever be, truly isolated. We are afraid of this inescapable "other," the "not I." Were this not the case, our fear of the dark would not be so universal, for the immersion in darkness can hold no terror for a truly solitary being.

This conclusion is not meant to be apocalyptic. We do not believe there to be a conflagration right around the corner. America's destiny, it seems to us, is not catastrophe but mediocrity. America has become luke-warm, the worst of all possible conditions. Neither hot nor cold, and it seems that God would have us be one or the other. Regardless, both conditions require courage. Lukewarmth is cowardice. This is a call to courage—the courage to be Catholic.

---

[246] *Man and Technics.*

Made in the USA
Charleston, SC
15 April 2016